Out of My Hands

Out of My Hands

My Life and Work as a Healer

Allon Bacon

This book has been printed digitally and produced in a standard specification in order to ensure its continuing availability

Published by Antony Rowe Publishing Services in 2006
48-50 Birch Close
Eastbourne
East Sussex
BN23 6PE
England

© Allon Bacon 2006

Previously Published by The Aquarian Press under ISBN 0850309313

All rights reserved. Unauthorised duplication contravenes applicable laws.

ISBN (10) 1905200579
ISBN (13) 9781905200573

Printed and bound by CPI Antony Rowe, Eastbourne.

To all those wherever they may be
who place their trust in me
I dedicate this book
with grateful thanks.

Whether you invite God
into **your house** or not, no matter;
He is already there.
After Carl Jung.

CONTENTS

Foreword   9
Preface   11
Acknowledgements   13

1. Another Day, Another Healing   15
2. The Healing Light   37
3. Music in My Head   52
4. The Developing Circle   67
5. The Healing of Nellie Quinlivan   86
6. The Messenger from Spirit   90
7. My First Stranger as a Patient   106
8. How Does Spiritual Healing Work?   116
9. Down to Earth   132
10. More Aspects of Healing   149
11. How to Meditate and Some Suggested Meditations   172
12. My Story Goes On   189

Index   197

FOREWORD

SOME 25 years ago I was dragged reluctantly and disbelievingly into Edward Fricker's healing clinic – he was described on his card as the World Famous Healer, but this neither encouraged nor impressed me. My back was so excruciatingly painful after a fall, I felt too pain-sodden to object and had nothing to lose. Ten minutes later, after some gentle laying on of hands by Ted, I walked out completely pain-free.

After such a personal experience, and having witnessed so many others since, I could never doubt that there are people with healing powers which have nothing whatsoever to do with medical training. Allon Bacon is a perfect and very genuine example of this gift – what's more, healing energies vary and his are of the most powerful kind. It is also reassuring that, just as healers recognize no religious barriers, there are no creatures, four-legged or feathered, that healing hands cannot reach, soothe and so often cure.

Allon Bacon shares many of his experiences and beliefs in these pages – they are fascinating, his style flows freely and this book will, I'm sure, enlighten and enthrall all his readers.

Katie Boyle

PREFACE TO THE NEW EDITION

All copies of the first edition of *Out of My Hands*, published in 1990 by the Aquarian Press, were sold. So, apart from copies in public libraries and certain rare bookshops, it gradually became an increasingly costly rarity available only on the internet. Nevertheless, because it appears, much to my delight, that this book has slowly become an important feature in the lives of an increasing number of people, I feel, after many requests, encouraged to arrange a reprint. Here it is.

As we are living in a crucial period in the history of mankind on Planet Earth, when time is being speeded up and many essential truths are emerging and being tested, so I, amongst others, am being asked for guidance and solace. As many of my readers have requested a sequel to this book, I am also preparing a second volume about my life as a spiritual healer, medium, composer and painter, with the working title 'Out of This World'.

May you, my reader friends, move on in these challenging days with confidence, hope and, most of all, with the blessing of God. As always, *'Thank you, Father.'*

Allon Bacon

ACKNOWLEDGEMENTS

To Vivien Leigh for her undying loyalty.

To June Penn, *Star*-gazer who always believed in me.

To Patrick Heyworth and to Morton Puner for their literary guidance.

To Dr Harry Bound, MA, MD, FRCGP, for his help.

To Bootie (in the past) and to Dottie for their valuable secretarial assistance.

To John and Maime Andrews in whose Guernsey home I wrote an earlier draft.

To Helen Parnell, who understands, with gratitude.

To Tony Ortzen (editor), Pam Riva and staff of *Psychic News* for their interest and help.

1.
ANOTHER DAY, ANOTHER HEALING

ONCE again my healing hands were placed gently about the neck and back of another human being asking me for help. I had met Joanna Syms with her family whilst on holiday. This time she had made an appointment to see me as a healer. As she walked into my presence I could see by her body movement some hint of what her words were to confirm: 'Constant stiffness in neck, back, and shoulders. Occasional intense pain spasms which stop me dead. Getting out of a chair, or even walking, can cause me sharp restricting pain.'

I sat her on a stool facing away from me, the better to place my hands about her shoulders. Not yet thirty, Joanna, who worked in her father's transport business as well as being a local councillor, had suffered years of pain since falling off a horse and chipping both her pelvic and pubic bone. She had been carefully treated at a hospital in Swindon, near to where she lived at Calne. Then she was allowed home to be looked after by her local doctor on condition she went to bed for three weeks. Willpower had got her back to work on crutches for another two weeks and still in pain.

'Your hands are giving out an amazing heat,' Joanna said.

'The healing energy,' I replied.

With my hands gently about her back and neck I listened as she told me about another accident before the fall from the horse. In March 1978, nine years previously, she had broken her right collar-bone in a car crash. After medical treatment her collar-bone had healed, leaving her with constricted movement in her neck. With the accumulated symptoms of these two accidents the pain was considerable.

Prior to our appointment I had, as ever, made my preparatory meditations, raising my consciousness in the technique I had used these many years to tune myself into the healing power. I had learned long ago that the healing power is a force much greater than my own energy, and which, when conditions are right, is allowed to flow through me. On this occasion I could sense it flowing into the back of my neck, down my arms and out of my hands.

'That heat is really incredible,' Joanna said again.

After the healing she was to have her words put on paper and signed, something which many of my patients agree to do to help me with my ever-growing file of case histories. Joanna described the healing experience thus:

> I was apprehensive until I felt the warmth which came from Allon as he gently touched my spine. Then an incredible thing happened. I felt as if some force other than human hands compelled me to move my chin up and my head back as I found myself staring at the ceiling.

I had explained to Joanna that my inner voice had told me her back needed stretching but that I, as a human being, was not qualified to carry out such a manoeuvre. A moment later, as if some third intelligence had heard me, the stretching was to be brought about by a force outside of me. As I witnessed the happening taking place I gently asked Joanna if she felt comfortable.

The answer was, 'Yes, no problem. I'm fine.'

In her description later of the healing Joanna went on:

> I could not move further, nor was I distressed. My incredulity caused me to almost laugh, not out of disrespect but out of amazement at this unique experience. Shortly afterwards the same unknown force caused me to move my head in the reverse manner until my head was gently lowered to between my knees. I had stayed there for perhaps a minute when I was raised up to my previous sitting position. I found my neck and upper back were now completely free from the restriction I had previously suffered.

When I had touched Joanna's spinal column I had felt a distinct bump a third of the way down and yet another hard protrusion a few inches below. Joanna was also to refer to this in her statement:

> What is more, on examining my spine I felt the (top) bump had completely disappeared. After a few minutes more of Allon's healing hands lightly touching the area, the second bump went too.

Completely amazed, I returned to my parents and tried to make my father understand what had happened.

Her mother accepted the situation; her father was finding it more difficult to absorb at that time.

Because of a slight residual stiffness in her back Joanna returned for another healing session. She was to testify later:

Within five minutes of treatment my back was completely free of all restriction. At one moment my hip became hot and I felt a tingling in my right upper leg, which had caused me pain since my first accident. As Allon treated my back a crack went off in my upper back. On standing up I found movement was even freer and my spine now felt smooth. As with my first treatment, it had taken less than twenty minutes. Years of suffering was wiped out in minutes. It was an experience I had never thought possible. I was not frightened for a single moment, such was the confidence I felt in those healing hands. It was so unbelievable that I can understand the sceptics. I was a sceptic before, but not now. I fully believe in the wonderful power of spiritual healing. How could I not?

After Joanna Syms had left my presence, I gave thanks that once again I had been used as the instrument for the healing power to lessen the suffering of another human being. I remembered once again how I had learned about my healing gift, by first saving my own life all those years ago. What better education for a healer than to have to learn first to practice upon himself? Such was my destiny. At the time I did not realize where the experience was leading me. I only knew that at the age of seventeen, whilst still at university as a first year medical student I had fallen desperately ill, an event which was to alter the course of my life.

Seventeen is young to be threatened with destruction by illness. I remember lying in my hospital bed at Frimley sanatorium that summer during the Second World War contemplating my fate. This sanatorium was linked with its parent London hospital, Brompton Hospital, then and now the most famous centre in Britain for the treatment of lung disease. The sanatorium was placed in a green suburb south-west of London, surrounded by trees. Built in a huge semi-circle, one wing was for men and the other for women with the operating theatre upstairs.

In those days before streptomycin was available, tuberculosis was a killer. It was as dread a word as cancer twenty years ago. With tuberculosis of the lungs such as had been diagnosed for me, the prospect was grim. As I lay there, all around me I heard men coughing, then the inevitable rattle of the metal lid as they spat into their sputum pots. Mine was beside my bed on my locker, and every time I used it I thought I had coughed up another part of my life. Only those who have experienced the invasion of an illness into their body can know the feeling of hopelessness which can overcome the spirit should you allow it. As I lay in my hospital bed I made a vow with myself that I was going to fight, fight with every part of my mind and my strength to survive.

The sister in charge, a small, bustling, Victorian-like character in starched cuffs and hat, hated seeing me in my single ward.

'You're lonely in here, Bacon,' she popped in to tell me at least six times within my first week.

'No, Sister, leave me please.'

'You're brooding, it's sad for you alone.'

'No, Sister, I'm not. I like it alone.'

At last she gave in. What I could not explain was that it was the very loneliness I needed to survive.

Whilst all the other men I met in the X-ray room or in the corridors were talking about the physical details of their illness, the deaths of other patients, the havoc the disease caused in one's life or what was left of it, I didn't want to know. My instinct was to gaze out of my single room across the path into the woods behind. I watched the light of dawn gently illuminate the pine trees, and finally, at the end of each day, fade into the darkness gently lightened by neighbouring windows. For our windows stayed open day and night.

I slept a lot, and I dozed. I learned to float my mind away from the tales of thoracic operations (when the rib cage was sawn through), away from the talk of needles forced between ribs to drain away poisonous fluid. I forgot the news of the latest haemorrhage when some poor man spewed up blood as he sank into coma. I raised my mind up to link with the universal strength I sensed about me. I was, without realizing it, reaching up to the Cosmic Energy of the Christ Consciousness. I was reaching back into my soul memory to knowledge I had absorbed from previous lives. I was linking with the eternal me. I was switching myself from being hypnotized by the stark horror of my surroundings to the overall reality of Divine Strength. My first great lesson as a healer had started. And what greater challenge than first to have to learn to heal myself? What more dramatic a lesson?

The irony of the situation was apparent. Studying to become a doctor, I was instead the patient. And as the patient, I was, without even realizing it, learning to be the healer I was destined to become.

Prior to being struck down with tuberculosis I was busily engaged as a medical student in my first year of the five which stretched ahead of me at London University. Previously, at Rugby School, I'd passed the necessary exams. I was staring into a microscope at the cross-sections of plants in Biology, or cutting open the earthworm, the dog-fish and the rat.

When war broke out, as London University medical students we were evacuated to Birmingham and attached to the Queen Elizabeth Hospital. In the day we attended lectures and worked in the extensive laboratories. At night we tried to sleep as the camouflaged Naval gun hidden in a nearby park was wheeled up into firing position to add its thunderous crack to the groaning jerry aircraft and the staccato ack-ack fire. Land mines floated down in ominous profusion, one nearly wrecking Snow Hill station, and bombs fell too near for comfort. As the tempo of firing increased, sleep became spasmodic.

Holidays were spent in London where the bombing was stepped up, as was the pace of our night life. I was living in my mother and step-father's large house perched on Putney Hill complete with drive, garden and garage housing the Rolls and the Rolls Bentley. The two servants were not yet called up and the chauffeur doubled as the gardener. For evenings out in the smart West End my mother, ravishingly dressed and as beautiful as ever, emerged with my sister in her debutante evening clothes, myself in dinner jacket and my step-father similarly dressed before he too was called up. Together we drove through the bombs to the West End as we raved it up with the obligatory false gaiety to the strains of Ambrose and his band at the Mayfair or Carol Gibbons and his piano at the Savoy. The theory being that each moment might be the last, so enjoy it. Added to the fact that as the good life was expensive, it naturally had to be enjoyed.

As I spun around the floor clutching my girl friend of the moment I found that although life on one level was colourful, on another it was empty. But I was not yet to know why. I could not envisage a future trapped as I was in the money belt and yet I could not escape a merry-go-round which I sensed was soon to damage my mother's health as certainly as it was to damage mine. Having survived a pre-war winter ski-ing holiday at Suvretta Hotel, St Moritz, where our table was placed near Joe Kennedy's clan, and then a last term at Rugby, followed by the bombing of Birmingham, nearby Coventry and now London, it was not surprising that my health, delicate as it had been since bronchial pneumonia at the age of two, finally collapsed.

At the Savoy I was sweating as I danced. My naturally wavy hair went ominously straight, my appetite, much to the disgust of my step-father, could not cope with the expensive food and my energy was flagging daily. The night sweats which set in were alarming.

When I awakened with my pyjamas soaked in perspiration to the point that they ran wet, my medical student brother-in-law was the one to say, 'Allon, you must be X-rayed.'

My mother nearly fainted at the news. Tuberculosis was not a socially favourable disease. It was the poor who died of it, not the rich. Nevertheless I was forced to drop my studies and after an unforgettable day of being driven round seeking a bed in the over-crowded war-time hospitals, I was finally admitted to the sanatorium at Frimley Green, Surrey. There I found myself in my single room with its metal bed, surgically clean wash basin, and the ever-open windows of the stable doors looking out onto the trees. If the shock of having seriously diseased lungs was bad news, the peace of my small room was welcome. The man within me sighed deeply in relief and hope. For the while nobody but God could get at me. I felt safe in that knowledge. I knew I was to survive. Meanwhile my situation was precarious at the least.

After being X-rayed by the huge machine in the basement, and then having a blood test, I met Dr Wingfield, the Medical Superintendent, a kind, elderly man.

'Bacon, we're putting you on bed rest, anyway for a month, and then we'll see what else we can do for you.'

He spoke so calmly. It was only as I lay day after day alone in my room that the awareness of what could happen to me filtered through. In those days the alternative treatment to streptomycin was either rest, or more sinister treatment. Fellow patients gave me the grisly details. Phrenic crush was the mildest. This was when they pinched a nerve leading from the top of the chest. Next in line was the Artificial Pneumo-thorax, the collapse of the infected lung by pumping in air between the lung and its surround to rest it. If that failed, next came the dreaded thoracic operation when they sawed through the ribs and forced a permanent lung collapse. I saw young men turn old overnight as they suffled past my window bent and pale after the 'thoracic'.

'One day we will have the new drugs available,' Dr Wingfield told me on my second meeting. 'Meanwhile you lads show such courage.' His caring face told me the ordeal which faced us.

After the first few visits of friends I learned from their faces the seriousness of my predicament. My mother, exquisite as ever, tried to hide her pity as she gazed at me. School friends in shining new uniforms came to see me, excited by their new commissions. I longed to be in their place. Their war seemed glamorous and adventurous. My war was solitary, and totally unexciting. In fact many of them disappeared forever, sacrificing their young lives in the terror of war – heroes each one.

As I lay in my bed I did welcome the time to think. That was superb. I was off the merry-go-round of study, sleepless nights being bombed and the false gaiety of the London night-life. Only an occasional distant German plane disturbed our sleep at Frimley. I thought about my situation deep and long. I had time to consider the main events of my life so far. Who was I? Where was I going? Where had I been? What was important to me? What was happening to me? And, most important of all, where did I stand with my God?

I was probably conceived in Barcelona. My father, Roger Bacon, had been working there managing some food business to earn a living whilst reading law. We lived in a modest villa on a hill behind the city where my sister was born. My mother hated everything Spanish, and my father worshipped it. Not a good start for a marriage. My parents, both intelligent and handsome people, had fallen in love as a preface to disaster. My mother, in a rare moment of intimacy, told me years later that she knew after ten days her marriage had failed.

To start his dinners at the Bar in London we moved to West Hill, Highgate, where, prematurely on Christmas Eve, after a troublesome time, I was born. My first memories are of our next house in Marlborough Hill, St John's Wood, with the mulberry tree in the garden and the tortoise. Here I grew up with a handsome young governess, Ruby Bartlett, whom we called Nanny. Our chief playmate was Prudence Leith-Ross who lived opposite and whose father worked in the Treasury. One of our other friends was Faith Brook, whose father, Clive Brook, was an international film star. She herself was to make the theatre her career. I remember Prudence's brother had built an early television set which I was allowed to see. As we gazed at the spinning wheel of lenses, blurred images moved before us in a magical way. It was explained to me that these images came through space. This impressed me tremendously.

The other images I saw as a boy danced on the ceiling from the oil stove as I waited to sleep and turned into faces. Was this early psychic awareness manifesting? As I slept I left my bed sometimes and floated up through the ceiling, my nose almost touching the cold brickwork outside as I rose up. I flew for miles, but on awakening could never remember where I'd been. I had a faint unformed memory of meeting with friends I loved somewhere else.

In terms of this world I was also fascinated to meet the lovely Merle Oberon, later to become Lady Korda. As a barrister my father acted for her in a law case concerning hair dye. To meet one's first film star in one's own home caused me also to dream of having some activity in the theatre. Actor? I toyed secretly with the idea. My love for the theatre was manifesting – but so was my early psychic awareness.

Known as 'Dreamer', I was a painfully thin and shy child with huge brown eyes. I suffered meeting strangers. I was happy in my world with my governess and my dreams. I spent hours in reverie in my daily routine of meals and walks. I created a private inner world peopled with my private visions. I knew from the start that some curiously special life was awaiting me, but did not know what it was.

As I grew up and my father took me about the art galleries, the vast religious paintings of the saints affected me deeply. I wanted to share their suffering and their saintliness. I understood them. I could not say that there was any heavy religious atmosphere in our home. At the predominantly Naval prep school I attended in Southsea, prayers were a part of the daily routine as were lessons and early morning swimming. I wondered why I heard my mother's voice calling my name when I knew in fact she was in London, or South Africa. Then I learned to accept my ESP experiences as natural.

A great periodical treat was to jump into a taxi with my beautifully-dressed mother and my sister Patsy, and visit my great aunt, Lady Marie Hall. Auntie, tall and gracious with the sweetest of manners and huge lovely eyes, was the widow of Sir Harry Hall who had interests in South Africa. My mother and Auntie would take off every winter on the Union Castle Line in their luxury suite, dining, naturally, at the captain's table. Auntie would regularly win the fancy dress ball competition as she had a copy made by Bermans, the best theatre costumier, of an elaborate costume from Chu Chin Chow, the great past musical stage hit. After the death of Great Uncle Harry, Auntie sold her country estate and moved into a suite at the Savoy Hotel, London. So our great treat was to visit. Daisy, the maid companion, who had eyes which looked in different directions, took us children to the kitchen which also looked out onto the Thames side entrance of the hotel. We ate cherries and dropped the pips onto the large-hatted ladies as they stepped out of their cars, then we hid as they looked up.

Auntie always dressed at Bradleys of Bond Street, London, who made her beautifully embroidered day clothes and long evening gowns dripping with beading and fringe. She was furious one day when the management of the hotel, whilst redecorating, asked her to move out of her suite to accommodate the visiting Mae West, who also loved the Savoy. Auntie moved out and never went back. She bought herself a flat in South Audley Street, Mayfair. Before she signed, she and my mother with permission moved in for the night with portable beds, a large picnic hamper, several half bottles of champagne and their initialled bed-clothes to test the bedroom for noise. Satisfied, Auntie moved in. An operation for cancer had not daunted her, as champagne was recommended as medicine by a caring doctor. Up to her death she was to send me letters at school with a pound note always included – a fortune for a boy's tuck shop then.

As for Mae West, I was to hear a lot about her from a distant cousin of my mother's, Mai Bacon. Mai had years before caused a stir in the family by running off to join the chorus at the famous Alhambra Theatre, London, which was well known for its musical comedies, and she rose to become a big musical star. As a man I was later to meet her back stage, away from the family background. Delighted, we were to swop family gossip. She was to tell me about the time she worked with Mae West in her famous show *Diamond Lil* which played the Prince of Wales Theatre, London, before touring the provinces. Mai Bacon got to know Mae West well, and was to tell me fascinating stories about this legendary figure.

Contrary to the flamboyant public figure she manufactured and projected, Mae West was in fact a very caring, rather diffident woman living by high ideals. Neither a smoker nor a drinker, she had a deeply religious side to her, studied the Bible, and was intensely interested in Spiritualism. I was later to meet Leslie Flint, the well-known direct voice medium, who told me that he held séances for Mae West in Hollywood when he was lent a flat in one of her properties, and at his old London home, and at the Savoy, possibly in the very suite once occupied by Aunt Marie, that she so liked with its view of the Thames embankment.

Another treat as a boy was when my mother took my sister and I into central London to visit the great new store, Selfridges. Gordon Selfridge, an American, was pioneering when he gave Oxford Street this vast shop. The clock was copied from a detail of St Peter's, Rome; the bronze-covered lift doors are now in the Brighton Museum. But it was the milk-bar which pleased my sister and I as we sat guzzling the latest fad – a milk shake chosen from the many flavours available. Then we went to the record department and joined in the fun as our mother chose all the new theatre hit songs. My first great love was *Show Boat*. I would sit listening at home for hours with my head in the loudspeaker of the wind-up gramophone as I lived the show. The world of 'make believe' became a real escape world.

It was no secret that Gordon Selfridge shared one of the famous Dolly sisters as a richly-kept mistress. She sometimes was seen rushing across London to her other patron, Aby, changing her jewellery on the taxi ride to please her appropriate lover.

Uncle Aby, as he was known to me, had a huge rich house on the edge of Regent's Park to which I was walked by my governess as a younger boy. I spent part of the day having lessons with another governess appointed to Uncle Aby's son. At Christmas we had to put on a show, being rewarded with a suit of armour or a full-size Punch and Judy show as presents. The girls downstairs who were invited to cocktails as we left were given real jewels which hung unwrapped but labelled on the vast Christmas tree. Uncle Aby was a friend of my Grandfather Sydney, and was to build one of the finest cinemas in London.

He adored my mother, as everyone did, and lavished gifts on her, some of which we were not supposed to know about. With his paunch, his silk suits and his huge cigars he was the sort of larger-than-life figure that fascinated. Later he was to give me a silver watch at school which I treasured.

Home life in St John's Wood soon came to an end as my parents grew more and more apart. A stream of handsome young beaux carrying flowers and chocolates were always coming to tea or cocktails with my mother. Then one came more than the others. In retrospect he was like Rhett Butler from *Gone with the Wind*. His dashing exterior hid strong inner drives. He was to carry my mother off and marry her. From then on my life was divided into two.

So by the age of twelve my sister and I had two homes, two addresses, two telephone numbers and two lives.

We spent half the school holidays with my father at his new villa-type house in St John's Wood, northwest London. The house was cold and we were always being told to turn off the lights to save electricity. I had to work in the garden helping with the new pergola or making the pond.

The other half of the holidays we spent at Putney Hill, southwest London. My step-father was a heavy-drinking, rising business tycoon. His father, later to be knighted, had built up with immense energy and acumen one of the largest businesses of its kind in the country. He was grooming his son, my step-father, to take over. Both lavished gifts of jewels and furs on my mother. She lapped up the new life like a starlet. She never lost her spiritual intensity, which emanated from her like a thousand-watt bulb. But if the truth has to be told, she sold out a part of her peace of mind for gold.

Life with mother was endless chauffeur-driven shopping sprees to the West End in the new Rolls followed by a theatre matinée or a film. Holidays were spent tearing about Europe in my step-father's white Rolls with Gibbs at the wheel. Home life was riding on Wimbledon Common or cruising up and down the south coast in my step-grandfather's yacht which had a crew of twelve and a French chef. My cabin was carpeted blue with silver fittings. I wore a blazer and a formal tie for lunch and we sported dinner jackets for the evening; the ladies wore beach pyjamas for the day and full evening dress for supper. When she wasn't at Ascot, my mother was filling up her wardrobe trunk to take off for the Reids Hotel at Madeira, or a weekend at Le Touquet or a quick dash to New York. On every occasion she appeared dressed like a dream, giving out tips, sweetness and love to everyone. I wondered where she found the energy. The answer was that soon she didn't. The charade of hiding her husband's heavy drinking from his father, and encouraging him through his tough actuary exam, as well as accompanying him to the nightclubs and city dinners was beginning to tell. She caught a cold in St Moritz and coughing and asthma started. Soon it was long spells of illness interjected with astonishing reversals when she reappeared looking exquisite beside my step-father for another evening out. Only in her mid-thirties, the tragedy to come was beginning to unfold.

The other problem in my mother's life was that although my step-father doted on her and my sister, he couldn't understand me. Having already been confirmed at the Queen's Chapel, St James's Palace, my sister's season as a debutante was lavishly backed with a coming out party at Claridge's prior to her presentation at Court. So she followed the pattern set by my great aunt, Lady Hall, and my mother.

I was the thin young brother who struggled on trying to keep up physically with the immense pace of the social life and my studies at Rugby School with its strenuous programmes of rugger, swimming, boxing and tennis. I loved my time at Rugby where my fast-growing physique shot up to six feet, but willing though I was, my energy was flagging.

Then came the war. Overnight we British blacked out windows, taped the glass, sand-bagged our public buildings, dug trenches and erected our Anderson shelters. We became unified as civilians at war with the same purpose as our newly uniformed men and women; together with the factory and hospital workers, our single aim, as Churchill inspired us, was victory over Hitler and his powers of darkness. If nights on guard on the local water tower as school-boy Home Guards stole our sleep, weeks at

Tidworth Pennings as OTC trainee officers were tough but fun. The pace was fast. Entertaining young Prince Philip of Greece, later to become HRH the Duke of Edinburgh, rubbing shoulders with the Mountbattens at charity functions, and on one occasion spending the night at the Mansion House, invited to a family ball by the then Lord Mayor of London, Sir George Wilkinson, was fascinating. The nightly bombing of London did not stop our partying. Falling ill was less fun. One moment I was dining in a tail-coat waited upon by uniformed Mansion House flunkeys under the bomb-shaken chandeliers, the next I was eating hospital food served by starched-cuffed nurses. The contrast was evident.

In my hospital bed two main thoughts occupied me – my future, and my prayer life.

My mother's family, also curiously enough called Bacon, had been steeped in the theatre. My Grandfather Sydney, had been a highly successful owner of a string of cinemas, and his father, James, had been an owner of theatres. So the entertainment business was in my blood. My mother always tried to play this down, but you can't fight chromosomes. Besides, because of her beauty and the constant interest it attracted, she had herself made a film, using Patricia Allon (my sister's name and mine) as her stage name. Filmed in St Moritz, the story insisted she sped down the famous and dangerous Cresta run, held tight by her burly hero. The Cresta, hitherto a man's world, was especially slowed down with a layer of snow for the occasion. The film was never distributed and lay disintegrating in a huge tin box in the attic.

On my father's side, Grandpa Sewell had been a successful owner of a well-known clothes and material store in Liverpool. At fifty he retired to become a very good painter. So this was in my blood too.

The later introduction to the highly-powered business life of my mother's new family by marriage left me cold. I was offered an entrée into it by my new step-grandfather if I chose to change my name. Much to his astonishment as I sat with him in his Royal Thames yachting cap in the bridge room of his splendid motor yacht I turned the offer down.

'Why, my boy?' he said kindly.

'Because I do not see about me many happy people,' I replied, to my own astonishment.

He stared at me for a full moment before he answered, 'Well, my boy – you've got a good head on your shoulders.'

Without my realizing it, the greatest influence on my spiritual life had been my father's mother, Grandma Charlotte. Of middle height, with immense brown eyes which saw into your soul, she was a deep thinker, and had written a book on philosophy, theology, and healing called *Infinite Traveller*.* She told me stories of communication between this world and the next as if they were the most natural of happenings. Our correspondence whilst at Rugby was of great value to me. Whilst never trying to influence my religious convictions she encouraged my prayer life. As I had a good singing voice I was placed immediately in the choir at Rugby. My confirmation by the Bishop of Coventry had meant a great deal to me. With Grandma Charlotte, a member of the Society for the Study of Psychical Research, as my first spiritual mentor my awareness of this and other words was wonderfully encouraged. I knew that in that area of thinking there was a vast treasure I had only just begun to unwrap.

My father too had written books and plays. As a young boy my playmates had been the Basil Dean children who lived opposite my father's second home in St John's Wood. Dean, later Sir Basil, a well-known producer, was to produce a play of my father's in a try-out production. Again theatre in the blood.

But what to do with my life? I'd chosen medicine because I'd always wanted to write and so many of the writers I'd read had started as medical students. Somerset Maugham and Chekov, to name but two. I also had an inborn desire to help people, particularly the sick. Little did I realize that instead of being the medical student studying the patient in the wards, I was to be the patient. As I lay in my hospital bed I wondered deep and long about my future. I knew I had reached not only a physical but also a soul crisis.

As bed rest had not worked sufficiently in my favour the verdict was an Artificial Pneumo-thorax, that is, I had to have my lung collapsed. I dreaded the day. Finally I heard the trolley approach. I was listening to some beautiful music on my radio and as matron bustled in and switched it off I thought of her

---

* Charlotte Bacon *Infinite Traveller* Williams and Norgate Ltd, London, 1939.

insensitivity in taking away this solace at such a moment.

As the sinister-looking lung-collapse machine was wheeled by the bed I tensed. I was proud of my young body, thin as it was, and I felt I was to be raped and scarred for life. I put my mind to neutral reaching up for help from any angels who would care to listen. As they bared my chest and laid me on my side I felt the cold swab of the spirit-soaked cotton wool. The crunch of the needle bearing anaesthetic was horrible. Then the swab again. The needle came out. Then a terrible pause. Then I glimpsed the huge needle attached to the air pump by the long red rubber tube. I shut my eyes and prayed as this cold steel object was forced into a space between my ribs. Then I heard an inner metal tube being withdrawn as the air was being let in.

'Breathe normally,' I heard the doctor say as my racing heart filled my ears with its drumming. I glanced up and saw a tear fall from the eye of my older nurse. This pity nearly finished me. I closed my eyes again. It was bliss when the trolley was gone and my bed tucked in.

'Good luck, my little darling,' the nurse whispered before she left me.

I was determined not to weep as the nurse had done. They'd given me a pill to swallow. Blissfully it brought sleep.

With my lung collapsed (Artificial Pneumo-thorax) I made progress. The dreaded trolley arrived every few days for a refill of air, and although I loathed it I held firm to my technique of taking a mental step up to ignore what they were doing to my body. I lived above it. Meditation inspired and strengthened by the trees about me continued to help me. I was learning every day to switch my mind to positive and grab at the Cosmic energy about me. The more I studied this technique the more fulfilled I became. Within the confines of my white room with its chair, basin and my locker, I was finding another extension. This brought me peace and even joy. After the initial rape of my body by the big needle I had learned to take a spiritual tranquillizer called 'The peace that passeth all understanding.' I was learning to be with Him.

When other inmate friends I made came to visit with their horror stories of ribs being dropped into buckets in the operating theatre and lumps of blood like red clotted cream being spewed out, I closed my mind to them. Reports of hilarious night ward parties made me laugh, and this was painful. Much as I appreciated the comradeship of my fellow patients, I secretly longed for them to leave me with my peace. I often slept deliberately through the morning visit of the doctor and ward sister, so that I did not have to be reminded again about the physical details of temperature, sputum, bowels, X-rays and my AP. To live it was enough. I floated on in my self-made dream world where I was finding a strength I knew would pull me through. The one aching question was, through to what?

The doctors were already beginning to prepare me for a whole new and different life when and if I survived hospital. It was general talk that socially TB patients were half way to lepers. Even some of my relatives smoked incessantly when visiting and stayed against the far wall in their obvious fear of contagion. The men told me of heartbreaking stories of love affairs cancelled, brothers eschewing brothers and marriages falling apart. Sports, sun-bathing, too strenuous activity of any kind was to be banned to most of us; that's if we were to survive. I was to look forward to a half life, it seemed, should I survive. And was I to continue my medical studies? The subject had not been discussed. The immediate struggle to rise from my bed was enough. But the subject started to gnaw.

I realized as I mused on my future that something intrinsic was happening to me. Whereas before my illness I was studying every aspect of the human body to prepare myself to be a doctor, now the reverse was happening. To fight my way out of my present predicament I was teaching myself to ignore the dictates of medicine. True, I was grateful for the tender care of the doctors and nurses. But I sensed that the real source of any future positive health was to come from myself. So if I was to survive by rejecting the medical prognosis laid down for me, how could I then plan to impose upon my future patients the same medical rules? Allopathic medical training was the exact opposite to the metaphysical attitude I had adopted to save myself. I was thus, as a future doctor, at war with myself. The physical details of the terrible illness I was witnessing slaying the men about me was revolting me. I was becoming over-sensitized to the gruesome and the tragic. I was fast approaching an identity crisis.

One night I had a dream. It followed soon after the original collapse of my lung when I was feverish and in pain. In my dream I was approaching a beautiful calm river winding below the green bank I was slowly descending. There, only a few yards below me, was a small boat tethered to the near bank. I knew it was my boat, waiting for me to use to cross the narrow river below me. In view on the far bank was a collection of men and women I longed to meet. Their robes were of pale bright colours and a soft yet brilliant light played about their tranquil selves. As I stepped down towards my boat a man's hand was placed upon my shoulder. A deep but tender voice said to me, 'Allon, you cannot go. There is work for you here to do.' I tried to see the man who spoke thus, but could only glimpse his linen robe. It was as if his face was purposely hidden from me. But such was the authority of his voice, I obeyed and turned back. There was great sadness in my heart as I climbed slowly back up the green bank. On waking this dream had affected me deeply. Yes, there was work to do. I knew now I was going to live. But what work?

After another few weeks of bed rest punctuated by the dreaded trolley and the refills, I was allowed to sit in the chair beside my bed. Then I was allowed 'basins', that is, I had to clean my own basin with cloth and cleaning powder. I made my taps shine like lighthouses in my joy at being on my feet. There came the great day when, on rather wobbly legs, I was allowed out into the sanatorium grounds. Then I was allowed one round of the circuit through the trees. Then two. Gradually my tired body was coming back to life. The women exercised too. At certain places our separate rounds nearly touched as we gazed curiously at each other's faces and bodies. I was tottering slowly back into a form of life. The present crisis was over. I was going to leave the sanatorium alive. I couldn't think further than that.

A few weeks later as my taxi took me towards the train for London I felt like an alien re-entering a strange world. I knew, as I approached my mother's home on Putney Hill that life was never going to be the same again. But just how different I could not have possibly guessed in my wildest dreams.

If I had known about the events to follow, I would have had a relapse there and then.

London, as well as other towns in Britain, was still being attacked by German bombers; the almost nightly blitz went relentlessly on. Frimley had meant a respite from the noise which damaged sleep. Returning to Putney was therefore, to step back into the stress which had been partly responsible for my illness. Our daily life was punctuated by the wail of the siren warning us of the immediate air-raid – to which we learnt to pay scant attention. Taking shelter in the garden's newly-built mini-bunker was soon abandoned as being too damp and dicey for health. We risked a more comfortable demise.

Whereas in the sanatorium I had had endless hours for meditation, now I was back facing the growing illness of my mother. She was spending increasing energy to present to the world, even under present war conditions, a perfect marriage. She had managed to keep my step-father on course in the office where he had risen to being on the board and the apple of his father (the Chairman's) eye.

My relationship with him was growing steadily worse. It was bad enough previously whilst being partly away studying for my career. When I broke the news that I did not want to continue with my medical studies the situation grew worse. My mother had done everything to try to link her husband and myself. Since I had my own room at the top of the house I was at least able to escape his occasional aggression. When, still a boy, I had been sleeping in his dressing-room, he would sometimes waken me in the early hours on his return from night-clubbing to try and wrestle with me. When he became too physical I realized there were forces within him which scared me. I'd never broached these fears to my mother. But when he stumbled out of the room to close the door on my mother's bedroom I felt relieved for myself but uneasy for her.

Twice my step-father had crashed his car with my mother in it when he had insisted on driving back from a night club in the early hours. On the second occasion he turned the heavy Rolls Bentley over, putting my mother, badly concussed, into Charing Cross Hospital.

Every ten days or so I had now to return to my specialist, Dr Young in Weymouth St for my lung air refills, screening and blood test. For two days afterwards I always felt unwell. But that, and my prayer life, was my life line.

My father had once more entered the army and in his legal capacity was becoming a JAG (Judge Advocate General). He had remarried and was stationed at Filey, near York. My step-father was soon to follow him into uniform and have a series of stationings mostly near Bradford. When well enough, my mother would visit, staying at the nearby Railway Hotel. The servants had been called up so that the house was often gloomily empty.

I worked part-time for Lady Churchill's 'Aid to Russia' organization from the Red Cross headquarters in Victoria St, packing up sea boot stockings to hump in bales across to the Army and Navy Stores where they were crated up ready for the merchant ships leaving London docks. Lady Mountbatten, who supervised our work, often appeared, elegant and efficient. When my call up papers arrived I stood in line with a batch of other half-naked men in Richmond town hall.

'Your war is to stay out of hospital, my son,' the examining doctor told me. 'Keep the beds free for the wounded soldiers.'

I was given the lowest of medical categories, grade three, and told to go home.

By chance I learned that a professional company of actors had opened in Rugby School to help entertain the war-weary civilians. Yvonne Le Dain, the director, had once produced me in an amateur production there and said if ever I needed work to contact her, so this I did. Thus I joined the company, having to get back regularly to London on the milk train for my lung refills before returning for morning rehearsals. We did a new play every week and the pace nearly put me back in hospital. But somehow I survived. I was glad to be working and to be away from my mother's anxiety for me. Entertaining the war-weary was new and exciting. I was learning to overcome my innate shyness, to develop my voice and to learn about presence on the stage. All this was to be of immense benefit to me years later, especially for media interviews and lectures on healing.

In between the first successful season and the next, I was back in Putney. My mother's health was deteriorating fast. Her terrible asthma attacks were increasing. Somehow she managed to rise from her bed and look beautiful to escort my officer step-father on leave. I hated to see her drain her frail energies accompanying him to night clubs. My relationship with him now was so bad my mother arranged for me to sleep out at a dingy guest house nearby when he was on leave. This wounded me terribly, but for her sake I agreed.

Once, alone with me in the house and suffering an asthmatic

crisis, she passed out in my arms and I thought she'd gone. I held her tight as I rang for the doctor. I realize now my desire to heal her saved her.

After months of nursing my mother it was agreed I needed a rest, so I went up to stay with my father at Filey. I'd placed my mother in the University College Hospital, leaving my step-father finishing a short leave at Putney. As I bid her *au revoir* she was sitting up in her bed, her lovely face immaculately made up under a white bandeau about her head. An inner radiance made her look incredibly young.

'Al, darling, I want you to tell me the truth – was your step-father home last night?' she asked me with a sadness in her eyes I shall never forget. It was the first time she had posed such a direct question. I could not lie.

'No, he went out on the town and didn't return until eleven this morning,' I answered.

'Those hostesses – I never knew where he took them,' she said sadly. I kissed her goodbye to rush for my train.

During my stay I suddenly felt very depressed for no apparent reason.

Ten days later it was agreed I should return to collect my mother with the chauffeur and her Rolls. I returned to London by train and made my way back to University College Hospital before telephoning for the car.

'Yes?' said the curt lady at the reception.

'I've come to collect my mother,' I said giving her name. The woman repeated the name and thumbed down a list.

'She died at twelve o'clock – half an hour ago. You'd better see the sister in charge.'

The words hit me like a bullet. Dazed, I walked to the lift and found the floor. I remember a kindly sister giving me a glass of water.

'Her body is in the chapel. Do you wish to see it?'

Hardly able to speak, I shook my head. My mother, only in her forty-first year, had gone from this world.

I made my way back to Putney where the house was empty but for the kindly Mrs Mackay. She had been our sewing lady for years and recently had showed up again to give occasional help to my mother. Although her consumption of cigarettes and Guinness in that order amazed me, her heart was golden; and quite by chance her husband was assistant at Hammersmith mortuary. In terms of my mother's body, she took over. I contacted my step-family in their huge mansion nearby at Roehampton, placed an announcement in *The Times*, and ordered the funeral. I remember not knowing whether to have a lead-lined coffin or not; it all seemed so unreal.

The following day the telegrams and telephone calls started in an increasing flow. My mother's body was by now lying in its satin-lined coffin on the dining-room table. I was too scared to go in alone so I peered first through the serving hatch before I entered. My mother looked like a beautiful life-size doll. I had never realized how still death was. Her eyes closed, her hair coiffed and wearing make-up she looked uncannily real. And yet she looked totally dead. As I gazed I saw her lips were slightly parted and a large fly hovered about her mouth making the sound as if she were trying to speak. I brushed it away.

As it was September, I'd picked a rose from the garden which I placed in the top of her apricot coloured nightie. I was too scared to kiss her and too shocked to weep.

When my step-grandfather arrived in his huge chauffeur-driven Daimler he went straight to his 'Babs', as she was known to her friends. Ten minutes passed before he emerged with tears streaming down his old face.

'And what about you, boy?' he asked. I shrugged my shoulders, unable to reply.

'You have plenty of determination,' he answered curiously as he left me.

My step-father arrived ashen-faced. He flew straight to my mother's body, demented with grief, pitiful to witness.

By that night I was alone in the house but for my mother's body and my step-father, who was drinking heavily. It was a living nightmare. As I emerged from the kitchen having tried to eat some snack, I heard feet creaking down the stairs. There was my step-father, stark naked, whisky bottle in hand, as he passed me making for the dining-room. As he swayed on his feet I followed him, fearful of what was in his mind.

'My darling Babs is dead, she is so dead ... so dead.'

He started to lurch over her body. As the hideous possibility occurred to me I placed a hand on his shoulder to prevent him falling over my mother's body. He swung round as I backed away. His gaze now fixed on me, I retreated to the door.

'Al, my boy, come here.' He gave me a tearful smile, his once handsome face showing tenderness. I stood riveted as he approached me.

'You look so like my darling Babs,' he muttered drunkenly as his swarthy arms reached out towards me.

Terrified and unable to cope, I fled up the stairs to my room. Pushing my large chair and a table against the door I lay down and tried to sleep.

My sister appeared with her new student husband. Their presence was comforting.

After the grand funeral at Brookwood cemetery in beautiful park land in Surrey, the smooth limousines carried the people, all in total black, slowly back to London. At home, my step-grandmother had already arrived to go through every chest and drawer and box room. She had locked everything possible before my step-father disappeared back to his posting.

'And what are your plans, dear?' her quiet voice asked me at breakfast.

'I'm not sure,' I stuttered.

'Because, well you see, dear, my son asked me to tell you we are closing the house in ten days' time.'

'And where do I go?' I asked, naïvely.

'He didn't say,' she replied, as she turned away to disappear behind another locked door.

Ten days later I'd put some of my few belongings into a friend's garage, packed a suitcase, and left, closing the heavy front door. As I climbed into a car with my sister to drive away from Putney Hill, I knew that chapter was over and that life as I had know it was never to be the same.

I was not yet nineteen.

2.
THE HEALING LIGHT

ALTHOUGH my mother left a request in her will that my sister and I should be cared for as long as we needed a home, in fact the opposite transpired. My sister, having married, did not need such sheltering; as for myself, what happened shocked me. Not only had I been made homeless, but my step-father made it his business to bring pressure on my sister's in-laws, who sheltered me for a few days in their lovely house in Surrey, to ask me to move on.

If I had been trained differently, and as strong as I am today, I would have contested the will. But the law was different in those days. I was to inherit funds from my grandfather's will when I was thirty. Meanwhile my step-father was to take the interest. He was earning a huge retainer salary from his father but it was to be two years before he handed me my own small private income, thus in fact saving himself super tax. My own resources were pitifully small as I once more left a comfortable house to wander. But where? I prayed for guidance as I took a train back to London.

I remember being in a slight daze as I put my suitcase into a metal locker at Victoria station. The effort of carrying it from the train had tired me. I went to the station canteen for a cup of tea and a bun. The place was full of men in khaki or blue uniforms looking fed up as they too rested from carrying their rifles and huge kit-bags.

A thin-lipped woman stared at me in my 'civvies' and non-military haircut as she said to her over-painted companion, 'He should be in uniform.'

If only she knew my longing to be strong enough. As I drank my tea my mind went blank. Then as if by some outside force an idea fell into my mind. I suddenly thought of my Aunt Gwen.

Gwen was the wife of my father's only brother, my Uncle Patrick, who was doing his military service in India. I remember she'd given me her card at my mother's funeral. Searching in my wallet I found her telephone number and rang her.

'Come to tea,' her calm voice said simply.

Taking the tube I reached Putney station but instead of taking the bus up to the big old house, I walked over a footbridge to the row of converted flats overlooking the river.

'Where are you living now?' my aunt asked me as I sat with her enjoying my tea.

'Nowhere.'

'Then take the studio couch,' she replied in her calm manner. 'You can pay me for your food.'

I relaxed as I looked around me. The large room with a gallery round the top had huge windows facing the Thames which flowed past the small garden below. Tug boats fussed by. It was a total contrast to the big dark house I had just left. I felt immediately at home.

It was to be my base on and off for the next year.

Our downstairs neighbour was a remarkable ballet teacher called Vera Volkova. Slight of stature, with her black eyes and scraped back hair Vera radiated vitality. Working in a disused chapel in the centre of theatre land, she received Margot Fonteyn, amongst others, for lessons. After the war, becoming internationally famous, she was to teach other great dancers who would fly in from across the world for just a few precious lessons, before she took over the Royal Danish Ballet Company. Having fled her Bolshoi training for the freedom of Europe, Vera was a dynamic and amusing woman who never tired of demonstrating, sometimes standing on the table, the differences between the East and the West in dance. During air raids we all shared the little shelter in the garden, where our gossip and laughter filled the damp gloom punctuated by the occasional crunch of falling German bombs exploding on nearby parts of London. I realized that I was drawn towards the company of creative people – that the force which flowed through them was akin to the healing power I was so determined to seek to strengthen me.

I found work as a film extra, though having to rise at five in the morning was tiring for my limited energies. I searched for work in the theatre but touring the agencies I met with no luck. I became depressed. I even tried for temporary work as helper in a canteen for troops – but my medical card denied me the chance.

Then I received a visit.

One evening alone in the studio flat in that half light which precedes sunset, I smelt perfume. It was Coty's *L'Aimant*, the favourite scent of my mother. Turning I saw her standing there. She was wearing a pale blue robe seemingly made of shimmering light. She looked radiant as she floated towards me, her presence filling me with calm.

'Hello, Al darling,' she said. 'Don't worry, I'm watching over you.'

I wanted to speak, but choked on the words. As I moved to embrace her she shook her head and disappeared.

This event affected me deeply. Later I was to recognize it as an important step in my psychic awareness. The courage it instilled within me led me to find work in Windsor repertory, at the famous Theatre Royal.

In this beautiful theatre with its comfortable dressing rooms I learned a great deal about stagecraft, which was later to help me as a writer, and I met such stars as Stewart Grainger and Ivor Novello. Playing parts in everything from Nöel Coward to Bernard Shaw led me to realize my talent and my limitations. The latter were exaggerated by my limited energies. Singing and dancing in revue was great fun. But I was only just surviving on my one collapsed lung. Finally my days at Windsor drew to a close. I was made redundant.

As my Aunt Gwen was an actress, understudying Fay Compton in the West End at the time, we both had our days free for job hunting.

We discovered also our strong mutual interest in all matters psychic. My visitation from my mother had led me to enquire into all the subjects pertaining to communication between this world and the next. With Aunt Gwen I attended many spiritualist meetings, asked many questions and read all I could lay my hands on. Some of the mediums we saw giving demonstrations were good, others less good, and some disastrous. The standards varied enormously. We visited all sorts of religious sects.

At one meeting belonging to an exotic group in some upper

room we were required to don long sari type robes and pray standing up. As the leader told us to face the East I caught Gwen's eye. Her robe was too short and mine too long. Starting to giggle we had to change and leave. Laughter overcome us in the street below as we staggered with stomach muscles aching to the nearest bus stop. That laughter was healing, a subject to crop up soon.

As I was still suffering a certain amount of pain from the enforced regular refilling of my AP, Gwen suggested I attend a healing session at what was then called the Marylebone Spiritualist Association. So one Tuesday I went to a healing session in their headquarters in Russell square. I was shown into an upstairs room and told to wait with a row of others on little wooden chairs. When my turn came I was ushered into the presence of a little kindly-faced lady in a white coat, protected by two screens.

'Sit down.'

To my surprise the lady spoke with a deep man's voice which had great authority and kindness. As I noticed her eyes were tightly shut I realized she was in trance state – something I had learned about recently.

'Belt too tight,' the voice said as I loosened my belt. 'Plenty of pain, yes?'

I told the presence of my collapsed lung and the pain.

'Quite, let us see if we can help.'

Firm loving hands were placed about my ribs. I can remember the comfort emanating from those warm hands now. It was soothing. I wanted it to go on for ever.

'My friend, I am glad you came here. For one day you will be doing this work.'

I nodded, amazed. To get well and strong was still my goal. Anything beyond the immediate I could not yet envisage.

'You will see.' The lady's head nodded.

I thanked her and turned to leave.

'Each night at ten o'clock link with us in prayer.' The man's voice spoke again from her. 'Because you are able, you will see the healing light. Goodbye, my friend.'

Years later I learned the lady was the great Nan Mackenzie whom I was to thank near to her hundredth birthday at the *Psychic News* dinner dance.

That night in the studio I waited quietly for ten o'clock.

Silently, as if switched on by some invisible hand, I saw as I gazed out at the dark Thames a light appear in the top right of my vision. As I moved, it moved, as if I was seeing it sideways, as it were. From then on every night at ten I was to see this light for years to come. Even if I was acting and standing before the fierce light of the stage shining in my face, I still saw the little circle like a golden coin glow for perhaps a second, perhaps longer. I thanked the spirit people for their help. For it was a link which strengthened me in spirit and slowly in body. I felt intensely grateful that I had found a path which I instinctively knew was essential and of ever-widening interest and involvement.

But in spite of the information given to me by Nan Mackenzie in trance, I could not yet accept the fact that one day I would be a healer. That was to unfold later.

In the meantime my energy was still well below par, but as my talents as an actor were not widely recognized, the parts I got were small. I could therefore handle them, just. I could not stand for very long without tiring, so I was always glad when the stage directions were 'Sit'.

My meditation and prayer life was still as important to me as ever, not only as a life line for survival but also because I sensed subconsciously there was much more waiting for me than my work in the theatre. Exactly what, I did not know. But I knew it would be linked with prayer.

Relations with my father since my parents' divorce had always been a little strained. I'd seen him in court in his wig and robes as a barrister, and knew that he brought home, both to his second wife and in the past when staying with him myself, a certain solemnity. With my sister he seemed more lenient. He had written me hard letters when I was ill, almost implying that my stay in the sanatorium was a minor annoyance rather than the crisis it in fact was.

After hospital he wanted me to work in a war factory as I could not join up. My doctor of course totally forbade this idea. At least my work in the theatre was spasmodic and allowed a siesta on non-matinée days which kept me going. Even when I was working for Ashley Dukes with Sonia Dresdel at the Mercury Theatre in a group of plays sponsored by the government in the form of CEMA, a body organized to bring necessary entertainment to the hard-pressed civilians, my father was adamantly unmoved. Dressed in the velvet and gold fineries of an eighteenth-century man about town, I played Witwood in Congreve's *The Way of the World*. All rigged out in his impressive JAG uniform with his red tabs and officer's cap, he came to see me act. Afterwards he took me back to his lodgings and spoke to me in hard terms.

I remember his service revolver lying in its leather holster on the table between us as he said, 'Allon, my son, if you continue to disobey my orders then you must realize I shall withdraw all support as a father.'

As his support had been financially nil since my illness, it was hard for me to grasp the implication of the words. I felt tremendously hurt and lonely at his total misunderstanding of my predicament. As I shook his hand and wished him luck I was glad to leave the cold stare from his elegant face.

I had auditioned at the Theatre Royal, Drury Lane, and had been accepted to join ENSA, an official organization for entertaining the troops. I had hoped vainly they might need me near London. In fact I was asked to join a group going overseas, and when the moment came for me to explain I was still living with the necessity of a lung collapse, I was naturally sent away.

My regular visits to my doctor were causing me more and more anxiety. He had been wonderful in accepting a mere token of the fee when he had learned I had lost my background. Through the last difficult years he had undoubtedly helped to keep me from the dreaded relapse which would have put me back in hospital. My trouble was that with each visit to him, the X-ray, the blood test and then the dreaded big needle, I was reminded of my illness. Away from this present reality, I could dream of getting better. There was therefore a conflict within. I wanted with the support of my healing light to find an area of peace without and within where I could grow really strong.

After one lung refill I fainted. The event alarmed me terribly. I thought for a moment as I lay on the doctor's couch that I was going to die.

That night alone in the studio I prayed for guidance. It was as if some inner voice spoke to me.

'Allon, you must give up your medical treatment and rely on prayer. We will see you through.'

I knew there was some spiritual back-up team ready to

support my decision. The calm and the peace this gave me was immense. My mind was made up.

Two weeks later as I presented myself to my doctor for the supposed refill, I told him of my decision. He looked amazed.

'Bacon,' he said, his kind eyes staring hard at me, 'do you realize once you let your AP go without refills that after one month the situation is irreversible?'

'I know, doctor.'

'You are taking a terrible risk. The only thing that could save you if you had a relapse would be the thoracic operation.'

I remembered the broken, shambling, young men aged before their years whom I'd seen tottering past my window at Frimley sanatorium.

'I am grateful for everything you have done for me,' I replied, quietly.

'At least I advise a phrenic crush.'

I remembered too this minor surgery consisting of crushing the nerve at the top of the chest.

'No, doctor, thank you. No more.'

'Then what do you propose to do about your health?'

'Pray. I shall pray to get strong again. Really strong.'

Dr Young gazed at my face long and hard. He must have seen some message coming from my eyes. He seemed reluctant to accept it.

'Very well then, Bacon. You'd better dress and go.'

As I shook his hand a few minutes later, I ran down the stairs and out into Weymouth St. I remember whistling as I walked. My tread felt lighter, my heart was full of hope. I knew I'd obeyed my inner voice and that the invisible powers about me would see me through. I knew also it was going to be a long and possibly perilous haul.

As my decision to cut free from my doctor's treatment had coincided with the arrival of a postcard from my step-mother inviting me to Cornwall, I acted on it. As my father was by now stationed abroad, my step-mother, herself going through difficult relations with him, was not afraid to back me up. She was in fact soon to have a painful divorce thrust unwillingly upon her. She saw the havoc my illness had caused to my energies and, thank God, had the common sense to ignore my father's blindness to my predicament. As I had also no immediate work coming up as an actor I was free to gather up my few belongings and take off for Looe. The train I travelled in was bursting with troops. We slept shoulder to shoulder through the night.

I had known Looe since I was six. With my father and my sister and Nanny I had spent a month there every summer, as a part of my shared time between my divorced parents. Later, after our governess left, we were joined by my father's second wife, a handsome ex-model girl who bravely took on her two step-children, with her charming if sometimes nonchalant manner.

We had always stayed with Mrs Hilda Toms in her small house facing directly onto Fore St opposite the old reading room with its sixteenth-century beams. Although my step-mother greeted me warmly, and although we were at first both lodging in the little house, with my young half-brother, we soon made a pact to lead separate lives. It was a perfect arrangement.

'You'm looking proper wisht, my little digger,' Mrs Toms said to me in her Cornish accent as I arrived early that morning on the single line train from Liskeard. 'What you need is a good stoggin' lining to your guts.'

With that she plonked down on her baize-covered table with its white cloth a great bowl of junket, a plate of soused mackerel, a country loaf and a dish of yellow Cornish butter. As the old photos of her relatives, the sea captains, stared down at me, Mrs Toms herself inspected me. She was a figure like Queen Victoria with her plump short body dressed in black and her white hair coiled up on top of her head with one huge single hairpin. Her ever-present companion, Leo the spaniel, slept at her feet.

The little house, two up and two down with its pink washed back yard and sailors' cabin room on the roof, reached by a long wooden ladder staircase up the back, was to be my home for three years.

As I had recently been a member of the repertory company at Windsor where I had also written some of the material for a revue, I decided that now was the time to continue to try to develop my writing talent, such as it was. So in between eating, sleeping, swimming and walking on the cliff paths I hammered away at an old typewriter given to me by my great aunt before I left Putney Hill.

When the day came that I knew I had passed the first month

since giving up my lung refills, alone in my room I knelt in prayer as was my custom. But this time I gave deep thanks for the relief of knowing the big needle was behind me. I prayed for growing strength and vigour and for the unfoldment of my spiritual path. I knew I had been led to Cornwall for the hours of contemplation I needed to nourish my soul.

I was winning my long fight for health when that first winter, I had a frightening setback. I had caught 'flu, which not surprisingly went to my chest. Feeling too ill to stand, I stayed in bed. Mrs Toms swayed upstairs followed by her dog and plonked a great tray of greasy food in front of me. I could only drink tea and take some soup.

The third night I felt terrible. Every joint in my body seemed on fire. My lungs pained me. For the first time since leaving hospital I was scared. The idea of having to go back to treatment with no-one to help me with the bills and no home to convalesce in, was frightening. I'd made the decision to go it alone, and for once I was faltering in my mind at the wisdom of it. I recalled Dr Young's words as I sweated and shivered. Finally that night I fell into a fevered sleep.

Then it happened.

I awoke to see two hands across my chest. Because the thumbs were together and the fingers pointing to my head I knew the hands were not mine. As I half opened my eyes I saw about me a group of people in white coats. To the right I saw my mother.

She spoke to me gently, saying, 'Al, darling, go back to sleep. I've brought the doctors to you and you're going to be all right.'

At this I fell straight back to sleep.

The next morning as I woke I felt the crisis had passed – I was tired, but just that much better. Within two days I was up and staggering about. Within a week I was out walking and fast getting back into my new form.

That spring I started to walk further and further. Then came the summer with swimming. I used to walk to a quiet cove, strip naked and, taking up a huge stone, exercise to strengthen my body. By the end of the summer I had grown out of my one jacket. My body weighed two stones heavier and it was muscle and not fat. I felt like a king. My spirit friends had led me through. I gave thanks for my deliverance, my heart filled with the joy of living in a young fit body.

My Cornish life gave me time for further development and awareness of my own psychic abilities. The whole atmosphere of the area, soaked as it is in the Celtic tradition, is thick with folk lore and stories of hauntings. Tales of headless horsemen and cloaked figures abound.

One winter's night, full moon and flood tide, whilst coming back to the house from the narrow alleyways of the cottages stretching down to the river I saw a woman standing in the neighbour's doorway. She was wearing a raincoat over a long nightdress, both apparently soaking wet. When I told Mrs Toms, sitting at the end of the corridor by her back parlour fire, she went visibly white.

'That's the poor woman who drowned 'erself these few years back on a night like this, flood tide and full moon. You'm psychic, my little dear,' she added as she stuck a hairpin into her chignon. 'That's what you are. Let's pick up and turn in.'

With that we both went upstairs to our respective bedrooms.

If the past made me aware of its spell in Cornwall, so did the present. I remember the first Christmas Eve I spent in Looe. Being my birthday, my mind naturally went back to the days not long before when I would be thoroughly spoilt with expensive presents. To shake off the past I wandered into a nearby pub just ten paces from my front door. The roaring fire lit up the men's faces as they sang carols. Then at closing time they wandered out, still singing, to climb into a fishing boat made ready for the occasion.

As the boat floated silently with the tide downriver the Cornish voices sang the carol *Silent Night* unaccompanied in harmony. The beauty of the music was superb. As I listened I gave thanks for the simplicity of my new life. If my future was uncertain, one thing was certain. I had time for prayer and meditation. I knew that would be my salvation.

Apart from the awareness of the earth forces issuing from the solitary or collective Dolmen stones I'd visited in Cornwall as a boy, the West Country had already been responsible for earlier events in my seeking for knowledge.

Once, whilst driving to the West Country we had stopped at Bath to meet a lady pianist friend of my father's, Carlyne de Lysle, who in my presence handed him a book saying, 'John asked me last night to give you this book.'

I happened to know that her husband, John Alleyne, had been dead some time.

It was in the car later that my father told me the fascinating story of how some of the famous ruins at Glastonbury Abbey had been located. John Alleyne, with his partner, Frederick Bligh Bond (See Bond, *Date of Remembrance* B. H. Blackwell, Oxford, 1918), had experienced a series of psychic communications including messages from a medieval monk called Gulielmus (William) telling them where to dig to find the missing Edgar Chapel which no one had so far been able to locate alongside the already excavated part of the Abbey.

A series of detailed architectural drawings arrived on paper with the same system, a kind of mediumship known as automatic writing. I had already seen one of these drawings in my father's house. When he told me that the people concerned dug in the required place and found the chapel, the story became acutely real to me, and when he later took me to the ruins and we examined the site, I marvelled. This was tangible and visible proof both for my father and myself of the reality of communication between this world and another time level, the one we have to die to enter. No-one in future could ever tell me that psychic communication was all in the imagination. Here was proof to the contrary, proof I could see, touch and examine. What was more, my father, with his legally-trained mind accepted it also. That for me was enough. I needed no more convincing.

On this return to Cornwall I now had the time for study. I borrowed from the library any books I could on psychic matters. Amongst the subjects I read about was psychometry. This process comes about when a sensitive or medium holds an object and opens up their psychic awareness to scan its aura. After experimenting, I found that a small object when held to my forehead, threw out images I could see on my third eye. This was located behind the centre of my eyebrows. Without even realizing it I was taking my first steps to developing mediumship. I knew that visions of my 'dead' mother had occurred naturally. This new experiment was brought about by a decisive act.

When I held certain small objects belonging to my step-mother sitting alongside the fire in Mrs Toms' front parlour, I described past events and people which she could agree to and identify. When later I was to stand in the caves burrowed deep into the cliff along the wild shores about us, and I saw mental images of wild men with casks on their shoulders, and hulls of ships crashing onto the fearful rocks of the shore so near, ancient tales of shipwreckers and smugglers came to my mind and my own imagination was triggered. Soon I was to start putting some of my stories on paper. My mediumship was being used for creative activity. I was learning to tap the mysterious world of a writer's imagination as well as develop my psychic awareness. I was also learning to distinguish between the two. This was to be of importance in my later development as a medium and a healer.

I had already had the great thrill of selling my first short story to *Argosy* magazine; sandwiched as it was between a story by Guy de Maupassant and one by Noël Langley, I thought I'd arrived. How naïve I was.

In between hammering out plays on my typewriter I had done a tremendous amount of reading. I became a postal member to Truro county library from which I borrowed and digested every book I could find on assorted religions. I studied Buddhism, Spiritualism, and all the other attitudes of belief I could find, seeking their similarities rather than their differences. I read the great philosophers as well as Adler, Jung and Freud. I then enjoyed studying the great diarists, Chateaubriand, Pepys and Dr Johnson. If I had been taught to study at Rugby, this was my adult education.

What personal philosophy emerged? In brief, I decided that as we live many lives on many levels of time our souls have to experience everything. We have to be rich, poor, to prosper, to suffer; we have to have white skins, black skins, to have known perhaps all the great civilizations of the past either first hand or by some other linking of spirit we might not yet comprehend. And one Divine Intelligence reigned over all.

'It is only by our hard times we grow – not by our easy times,' I heard my Grandma Charlotte saying to me. She was soon to die, but her influence lives on.

Over and above all the intellectual study, I was aware of my own inner experience evolving. I seemed to attend class in a sleeping state. My mother's bringing the spirit doctors had deeply impressed me. My own obedience when the voice told me to break away from medical treatment for my lungs had been so far proved right.

When now, a few years since this decision, I jumped on a train for London and went back to see Dr Young, he found my appearance hard to believe.

'Shirt off, Bacon,' he said calmly as I donned my robe to be screened, X-rayed and have a blood test. I dressed and waited for his verdict.

'I don't know what you've been doing in Cornwall, but according to my tests you are as strong as the next man.'

He looked at me as a proud father might his son. I thought he looked much older and tired and the room seemed smaller as my new wide shoulders pushed their way through the door and back into the world. I skipped for joy as I hastened away. A woman passing gazed at me in delight as her face reflected the smile on mine, and in my heart I gave thanks yet again to my guardian angels and whoever had been responsible for my deliverance. In spite of having lost my home and my background, thanks to my trusted inner voice I had been inspired to win my battle of survival. The battle of the big needle was over. I was ready for the future. As ever it held dramatic surprises.

Mrs Toms grew weak and ill and finally, whilst I was away on a visit to London, disappeared. She died with relatives nearby. She had previously promised me her house, much to my astonishment. But when it came to it, all I was allowed was to buy it. Since by now my step-father had at least handed me back my small income I thought he might lend me the money to buy the house. Like a fool I went to London to ask him.

As the war was now over I'd written to him first and he had offered to help. When I got to the huge office block in the City of which he was now chairman I was shown not into his office but instead into a small interview room. A shame-faced man handed me a letter saying that by offering to help me my step-father had meant he would pay for surveying the house.

I went back broken-hearted to Cornwall, kicking myself for having laid myself open to such deceit. He had always been jealous of my mother's love for me and this had prompted him to abandon me in the first place. Was that to alter now? He had always known that although my mother loved him, she never wanted children by him. I think this had hurt him deeply.

I had placed a deposit on the cottage out of my own money, and now with the kind help of a local solicitor I had to fight for this back. So the day came when I had to pack up my belongings and leave the little house. Once more I was homeless.

I stayed with friends in nearby Polperro for some time, taking a room in their beautiful house. As George Bray, the owner, was an antique dealer, I worked in his shop in the afternoons to help out, still hammering at my typewriter in the mornings.

'Tycara' was perched high above the little fishing port, with seagulls swooping about the windows. A lovely garden had been levelled off by Stuart Armfield, the tempera painter, who shared the house. Inside, Stuart's paintings graced the walls, punctuating the shining ancient oak, mahogany and walnut furniture. We dined on heavy brass-studded Spanish chairs pulled up to a refectory table in the hall, eating when entertaining off Georgian silver platters, the salvers glittering in the candlelight.

George, dark-skinned and handsome as his Spanish forebears, entertained with panache. My social life once more stepped up apace. Amongst many others we welcomed Eric Portman, the well-known film actor, who had a cottage nearby up the river from Fowey. At his place I met Lady Du Maurier, mother of Daphne, the famous writer.

We also entertained the attractive Daphne Bath, now divorced from Lord Bath of Longleat and married to writer Ian Fielding. I had met her and her young daughter previously in my local, 'The Fisherman's Arms', with its slate floor and polished beer barrels. Years later I was to meet Alexander Weymouth as a friend and neighbour in St Tropez; one of Bath's sons, he was to show me his lively murals decorating the private wing of Longleat. With his flowing hair, beard and bare feet, he is a wonderful host and a passionate Wessex man.

From Polperro we paid return visits to Prince Chulah of Siam's house at Bodmin where we were waited on by white-gloved servants. One evening I did psychometry on the Prince's ring at his request. After a series of pictures of ornate palaces and exotic plants I suddenly saw the picture go black. I felt embarrassed and disappointed. Within a few years he and his charming British wife were both to die young of cancer. I have never wanted to use my powers to foresee death since.

It was Eric Portman who said to me one day as we walked in the garden of his lonely cottage, 'Allon, you have a curious power of bringing peace about you.'

I did not at the time understand the significance of this

remark. I do now. Being an actor of great energy and sensitivity he had sensed my healing powers without using those actual words to describe it.

Later in his dressing-room in London when he played opposite Marguerite Leighton, I was to meet so many of the other great names of the theatre and film world, Danny Kaye and Terence Rattigan to mention but two.

Finally my typewriter hammered out a play which attracted the attention of a London try-out theatre, and, sadly, the time came for me to pack up my few belongings and leave Cornwall. It was hard to turn my back on my friends there and on the beautiful rocks and coves of that glorious county. As the train pulled out of Liskeard station I knew that a chapter in my life was over. I wondered what adventures waited for me in London. I was soon to find out.

3.
MUSIC IN MY HEAD

My first production, which opened at the old 'Q' Theatre near Kew Bridge at Richmond, was a great boost to my career as a writer, and to my morale. Donald Sinden, then young and unknown, was one of the excellent cast. I received some good reviews, particularly from the *London Telegraph*, and although I was not able to sell it to the West End, the play *Cry for the Moon* was subsequently performed in several repertory companies and broadcast in Australia.

In terms of my psychic awareness an event took place just before my play opened which impressed me greatly. As a result of meeting the stage star, Mary Ellis, in Cornwall, I had been introduced to the great composer-actor-manager, Ivor Novello. When I presented myself at the stage door of the Palace Theatre, London, after seeing him in his wonderful musical *King's Rhapsody*, he sent his secretary to greet me. Ivor remembered having seen me singing my own song in a revue at Windsor and when I told him of my play which was about to be tried out at 'Q' he said he would come and see it. As I left he called out, 'Goodbye.' It was then a most strange thing happened. As I walked out of the dressing room I heard his voice like an echo calling again, 'Goodbye.' I thought it strange he would call out like this to a comparative stranger.

The next morning I opened my paper to read, 'Ivor Novello Dead.' He had died opening a bottle of champagne whilst dining with Tom Arnold, his impressario and friend just a few hours after I'd seen him. It was a psychic friend who explained to me that what I had heard was his voice echoing across the Valley of Death.

Once again, recovering from the shock of the experience, I realized that as in the case of my mother's voice after her death, my link with the next world seemed to be growing stronger.

After staying with my sister and visiting friends at Camberley, I found myself once more without a home. London seemed to hold too many past memories to make me want a permanent home there. Having spent a weekend at Brighton and liking it, I decided to live there. I was by the sea, which I love, and nearer to London than Cornwall. I loved Brighton's vitality and elegance. I was soon to discover that many theatre people lived there. A whole new world of people and events were to be opened up to me.

Staying at first in a small hotel run by a very vital character who called herself 'Sunshine', I realized as I worked on a new script that the place was emptying about me. The fellow writer who had introduced me to it had left, and finally I was alone. As the furniture too started to vanish, I learned from the now tearful 'Sunshine' that her business affairs had gone awry. The bailiffs were in. She found a small flat for me nearby, and then disappeared. Those rooms were to be my home for the next decade and more.

Obeying an instinctive urge to travel, I bought a two-wheeled Lambretta 175 and a tent. As I had always longed to see the South of France, vividly portrayed by Somerset Maugham, I drove to nearby Newhaven, and, pots and pans and suitcase on the back, I caught the boat and made for France, where I headed south.

Meeting up with a group of students who were heading for the Ile du Levant, one of the Porquerol group of islands off Hyères near Toulon, I left my Lambretta on the mainland and took the small boat to the island.

As I put up my small tent on the edge of the azure sea I joined a group of sun worshippers and health fanatics. Soon I was learning about correct diet, rough brown bread, eating less meat and studying vitamins and food values. In those days of the fifties all this knowledge was new and revolutionary. As I started to work away at my French in between snorkel diving in the wonderfully clear waters, I tuned in once more with nature and felt the strength of the cosmic vibrations charging me. We all swam naked and wore the barest minimum in the tiny shack-like shops on the small island. I also met a Swiss/German doctor who, looking fifty, confessed to me he was over seventy. He taught me some calisthenic exercises, lectured me on bad eating habits and inspired me always to return to the sun and food of the Mediterranean where I would recharge myself after the dull skies of Northern Europe. It was a habit I was never to drop. But on my return to Paris something else occurred which was to extend my life in a manner I had not dreamed. Once more it was a psychic experience involving clairaudience.

I had written lyrics and sketches for revue material whilst at Windsor repertory. But the music was supplied by others. During a part of my stay at Looe, I had met a very glamorous lady called Thea who wrote some music to my lyrics. But Thea, although a delightful companion, was always more keen on her social life than working. Her father, Lord Instone, had started Instone Airways, later to be bought by Imperial Airways. Thea caught aeroplanes as we catch buses or the tube. After going nearly off my head waiting for Thea to step off her social round and work seriously, I gave up hope. I was hungry for work, but she was not. After some months of terrible frustration the desire to compose music was born inside me out of desperation.

At Rugby I'd been the despair of my music teacher as, eschewing the plodding advance I'd made in classical piano, I preferred to lock myself up in the practice room and hammer out the latest songs on the black notes only. My mother, who had her letters in singing, piano and violin, had brought me up with a wide range of music. 'Love it all, then wherever you are in life you'll be happy,' was her wonderfully wise advice.

I'd never been trained in composition. Then on that certain day as I stopped for a meal at a street-side restaurant in Paris with my belongings piled up on my Lambretta, parked under my watchful gaze, some music started to break in my head. It just arrived. I grabbed my pen from my shirt pocket and started taking some sort of notes on the paper tablecloth of my table. I started writing the lyrics which were born with the music in my head. I remember them now, all these years later:

> Oh, what a journey, darling, this has been,
> The wonder of the beauty I have seen,
> I've seen enough to last my whole life through . . .

By the time I'd got back to England the music and words were still coming. I rang up a musical friend asking for advice.

'You're a composer, that's what, and you don't know it. Get it onto paper.'

I found a notator, and within two weeks we had put a whole score on paper. Meeting by chance a certain J. Baxter Sommerville in the local theatre bar, I asked him if he worked in the theatre.

'I'm the Managing Director of the Theatre Royal,' he answered, looking like Mr Pickwick.

On telling him about my new musical, he auditioned me in the empty theatre the following day.

'That would cost thousands to produce,' he said. 'Put this to music.' He threw me a copy of T. W. Robertson's *Caste*.

As I read the simple story of the two Victorian officers and gentlemen who fell in love with two sweet girls from the other end of the Thames – the East End – my heart identified with their social problems. Within three weeks I had thumped out fourteen songs on the little second-hand ship's piano I had installed in my flat. The words and the music simply flowed from my hands.

When J.B. (as we called him) heard the music he was delighted, then complications, as so often in life, set in.

The details of what followed are not necessary for this page. Suffice to say J.B. had already contracted a director for a musical version of *Caste* who preferred another composer. So having been invited to write the music and then thrown out all in one breathless month, I was free to take my version to another management.

So the curtain went up on my show at the Connaught, Worthing, the same night as the rival production at the Theatre Royal, Windsor. *The Stage* reviewed us side by side and my press was as 'gay and witty as a new operetta'. The rival show never got to London. I had three offers in two days and we opened at the St Martin's Theatre, London.

The events of that first night are engraved on my heart forever. I can still see the pink billboards with snowflakes of a London winter floating over them as the big cars rolled up emitting the elegant first nighters. It was hard to believe my name was up there. *She Smiled at Me*, words and music by Allon Bacon.

It all seemed unreal as the orchestra thumped out the melodies which had delighted the provinces. The public at Worthing had voted my show the best piece of the year. Chappells had already published the music. Billy Cotton had agreed to an excerpt on television. We'd been interviewed on the Henry Caldwell Saturday night television show playing my number *Music Hall* which always stopped the show. Curiously enough my melodies had been greeted by the press as Novello styled. I felt a million dollars at that, and remembered my psychic experience before his death.

The superb arranger, Peter Knight, had done wonders with my melodies, which he loved, attending many rehearsals himself to get the best out of the pit orchestra.

Jean Kent, the film star, had been signed up for this production, but without consulting me the management had called in another writer to divide the show into two acts. My agent at MCA did not advise me to fight for my rights as it was my first London show. At the final try-out production I felt the charming simplicity and innocence of my version was being tampered with. During dress rehearsal in London an element of pastiche was introduced entirely against the sincerity of my version of the story. I felt ill-at-ease.

During the first act the famous impresario Harold Fielding was introduced to me as I sat in front of him in the stalls. He wanted to sign me up. I was too numb with nerves to say yes at that time as MCA wanted to keep me.

Then as the show unfolded I realized something was going wrong with the chemistry of the evening. *Music Hall* did not, for the very first time, receive its usual huge round of applause. My heart sank. By curtain down I knew something had gone terribly wrong. The stage management over-milked the curtain calls, which were warmly applauded. Then as Jean Kent stepped forward, a voice in the gallery gave her the bird. My heart bled for her.

The notices next day were poor. It was one of the cast who told me the worst when I called at the theatre two days later for my mail. The show was coming off after three nights. My brain had to accept the shock. I went back to my flat in Brighton to a telephone which was silent. A week before I had had the world at my feet, now I was out. I felt numb.

I prayed for guidance. My inner voice said, 'Write another show.'

Searching for another script for a musical I produced another one of my own. But I could not sell it. Then after a long period of frustration I happened to come across a copy of *The Importance of*

Being Earnest by Oscar Wilde. As I read the title page, a waltz was born in my head. I went to Paris to glimpse the hotel where Wilde had died, and, as if I was inspired by the city, I wrote most of the show there. It was so cold in my hotel that I had to walk about in between setting the lyrics on paper.

Back in England I finished setting the music and once more J.B. backed a try-out in his beautiful old Theatre Royal at Margate. The show, *Found in a Hand-bag*, was well received – but no London offers emerged. However, it was to have more productions and tours over the next decade.

So Paris entered my life. The city cast its spell over me, an influence which has never left me.

One of the most enthusiastic members of 'Hand-bag's' audiences, one who kept returning, was Jack Strachey, the composer who had written the standard hit *These foolish things*. He proposed me as a member of The Song-writers Guild, on whose committee he sat, and at his request I was present later when his wife, Bridie, saw him accepted into the Catholic Church – a moment of great spiritual significance to them both. Not many years were to pass before we celebrated his life at his funeral.

Another who enjoyed my shows was the writer Lord Robin Maugham. Nephew of the great Somerset Maugham, he had already established his own name since being blown up in a tank as a lieutenant in the Second World War during the North African campaign. Kept busy with his work, his social life and his travelling, he had a spiritual side known to few which led him to seek an answer to the divine mysteries whilst approaching Buddhism. He was interested in my psychic abilities, and urged me to take notes for use later. After reading the draft of a novel I'd written, he encouraged me to continue writing. He was interested to learn that in Cornwall I had disciplined myself to produce after reading his uncle's *The Summing Up* and *A Writer's Note-book*. Robin Maugham was to introduce me to the famous composer Sir William Walton who, with Lady Walton, was his neighbour on the Mediterranean island of Ibiza. Walton's conversation was as captivating as his music.

When later on as a healer I was invited to try to help Robin balance his diabetic problems, the restless conditions of his lifestyle were not to make this easy. His zest for life assisted him but it caused him to dissipate his energies.

Robin also introduced me to the legendary Noël Coward and so I had the chance to witness his abrasive and witty repartee first hand. It was to be years later, in 1984, when I was to attend the ceremony at Westminster Abbey, when in the presence of Her Majesty Queen Elizabeth the Queen Mother a memorial stone was unveiled in Sir Noël's memory. As his enchanting songs were sung accompanied by choir and orchestra, I thought of the many times I had worshipped in that setting as a boy with my father.

I remembered too how three years previously I had attended another memorial service in St Paul's church, Covent Garden, when Dame Flora Robson had read a portion of Robin Maugham's own autobiography, *Escape from the Shadows*, in his memory. I had kept my pact to him as, watching beside his last hospital bed in Brighton, I prayed that his vital soul should be released in good time from his comatose body to wing its way to start a whole new creative life in another world.

Whilst staying once more in my tent in the South of France, I became friendly with a group of young actors, and some show girls from Paris. They said to me there would always be a room for me in Paris. So one day, after parking my Lambretta in the street below I carried my kit bag on my shoulder up the five floors of the ancient oak staircase to the attic apartment of 31 rue de Seine, the house belonging to Raymond Duncan, the brother of the famous and outrageous Isadora. Hippolyte, the brother of George Sand, had lived there, lending his rooms to his famous sister. Her grey-suited phantom passed me on more than one occasion on the stairs to remind me that Chopin had once played the piano in the hall on the ground floor. The pit-a-pat of her leather-shod pumps announced her presence.

Raymond Duncan wore long, hand-woven, monk-like robes and, sandalled and long-haired, his imposing presence was often seen about the art galleries below.

We occupied three rooms. My metal bed, which cost one pound in the flea market, was placed in an alcove just inside the front door. Our toilet, decorated with a bust of Beethoven we found in a dust bin, graced the landing. A small shower fitted in a corner of the tiny kitchen off my room, which acted as a corridor, with an old window opening, as did the kitchen window, onto a central courtyard. The living room-bedroom was the third room, graced by a simple metal-fronted fireplace with a window facing the narrow, busy street below. This setting was to be my home whilst in Paris for a part of each year for a full decade.

My psychic senses responded to the cobbled streets of Paris, as history recorded in the ancient stones played itself back to me. My pen had already been busy, and so were my crayons and brushes as my desire to express myself in painting broke forth. The French love and encourage creative people in a way the British don't care to. I owe them such a debt. As I came and went between Paris and Brighton producing my words and music and now my paintings I managed to survive through many a freezing winter in that extraordinary city.

My increasing psychic awareness manifested in my reading hands as I sang for my supper in Paris. My prayer life was enriched as I meditated in the beautiful church of St Severin, a building I am convinced I helped build with my bare hands as a working stonemason monk in a previous life. I have made many pictures of its beautifully proportioned, mostly gothic interior, and it is a subject which never ceases to fascinate me.

Every night possible in Paris I bought a promenade ticket for a few francs at eleven o'clock to witness the extraordinary Edith Piaf living her songs. A great actress, she chose music as her expression because of her unique singing voice. A deeply religious woman, I was later to meet her. As she shook my hand, holding her arthritic fingers seemed like touching a wooden spoon. Her body, deformed with illness, was forgotten as she gave out a wealth of charm and even sex appeal. Years later I was to scramble over the tombs in Père Lachaise cemetery with thousands of others to pay my respects at her funeral. Her voice lives with us now.

If my life in Paris was never luxurious, it was totally fulfilling. I developed there on three levels, psychic awareness, form and colour, and music. Remembrance of a previous life ending on the guillotine, whose soul memory was bound up with the Revolution stirred me to write another musical. Never produced, the score still lies on my piano. But nothing is wasted, and my experience as a creative artist makes me a more understanding healer of men's bodies and minds. You cannot help others without past struggles, as the God-given energy to rise up and live on emanates from you.

St Severin, Paris, original 60×80 cm *(Ink and wash painting by the Author)*

As my many-sided life unfolded, I knew that something of enormous importance to me had yet to evolve. But what? My words and music had earned me a little, as had my painting. I'd met some fabulous people, and lived in many a colourful atmosphere. My psychic awareness was always developing, as was my prayer life. My health had gone from strength to strength. But I sensed deep within me that in spite of the colourful life I was living, that deep down within my soul were emotions as yet untapped. I knew I had to develop some God-given seed within me. Something greater for me than just creativity. I had yet to find it.

Meanwhile I was busy adapting a song from *She Smiled at Me* for Dora Bryan to use in her summer show at Bournemouth with Marty Wilde. Dora had become a friend. The song was then used in a touring revue for years, a show which played New Zealand after summer seasons with Jack Tripp at Eastbourne. My music was still alive – just.

In terms of encouragement to my creative career my father had already done an about turn. Now Sir Roger Bacon, Chief Justice of Gibraltar and then of East Africa, he had married for the third time and settled in his retirement home, a converted farmhouse sheltering under a tall mountain topped by a monastery. There, near Pollensa in Majorca, he had created an English garden in a setting he regarded as paradise. One day whilst holidaying near St Tropez in my tent I learned that he was ill. Rolling up my tent and driving to Marseilles on my Lambretta I took a boat to Palma, then drove along the long straight dry road to Pollensa. The white-coated servant politely hid his surprise at seeing the son of the master arrive in blue jeans with face unshaven. Travelling second class was not luxurious. As I was ushered upstairs into my father's large bedroom I saw his white groomed hair and his blue silk pyjamas. His gold pen and note block were laid on his polished bed table. He looked serene and surprisingly well.

'You look a bit scruffy, my son,' were his first words. Little did he know I'd only had the money to travel and sleep on deck.

That night as I bathed and changed in my lovely guest room en suite with bath, unseen hands took away my clothes to wash them as I changed into my whites.

As the day went by I had a chance to meet my father again. Illness had softened him.

'I'm sorry, my boy, I did not understand your past illness. Now I do.' In reply I simply took his offered hand.

My heart was full as he gazed at me with sympathy softening his stern look. He was to live another few years before a heart attack killed him on a visit to London to bury his father-in-law, Sir James Conolly, ex-Governor General of Western Australia. His memorial service, in the Middle Temple Church by the Law Courts, was of great dignity. Thank God we had made our peace. But what pleased me was that at the time of my father's death there was found on his piano a copy of my published music which he had learned to play and enjoy.

My step-father was to die suddenly later whilst asking his third wife for a whiskey in his London flat. I have long since made my peace with him from the 'other side'. I remember the positive side of his actions to us all.

Gathering some funds, I bought a tiny flat partly overlooking the harbour at St Tropez – a place I had visited and immediately liked.

Little did I realize that I was on the edge of a series of events leading me from the theatre into the further manifestation of my psychic powers. As I had not yet taken possession of my flat in St Tropez, I stayed as I had done so many times before in a secluded campsite four kilometres outside the town. Here I was following my daily routine of swimming, meditation and, being a holiday, enjoyment. The telegram from England cut short my stay. 'Vivien Leigh has read your play and wants to meet you.'

I had written the play *Point of View* the autumn before in Paris whilst trying to keep warm in our rooms in the rue de Seine. Now I was hurrying back to England having had my rewrites accepted by my agent, the great Curtis Browne. He had interested Sir John Clements (then just John Clements) who had in turn offered the play, as impresario, to Vivien Leigh. It was her mysterious star quality which caused us all to come running. Though her career had foundered a little since parting from the great Sir Laurence Olivier, her name could still attract the backing money needed to launch a new project. So I journeyed to meet her.

Following John Clements' car down the long straight Roman road leading to Blackboys in Sussex we turned left past the village down a narrow uneven lane. There before us appeared Tickerage, the converted old mill house standing by the old stream and lake, which was Vivien Leigh's beautiful country home. England had never looked more beautiful to me than when I saw the old red brick house in its green setting of lush grass and nodding trees fronted by a pebble-covered circular drive. Standing outside her front door, immaculate in a tailored costume of pale blue, with her dark hair perfectly arranged, was Vivien Leigh.

'Hello,' she said to me as I shook her offered hand. 'I'm Vivien Leigh.'

I laughed as I replied, 'I know that. What you don't know is that I'm Allon Bacon.'

She laughed as well, and at that moment we felt an instant rapport. If friendship can be born instantly, it was then. During the next four years our friendship never wavered in spite of what we were both destined to experience. For Vivien had that wonderful gift of making friends, and, once made, of holding them forever.

As I ate my lunch that first day I could hardly believe that the events were real. As she talked about the possibility of opening in London or on Broadway I tried not to show the excitement which was bubbling inside. All the years that I'd sweated away at my craft in the theatre were now paying off, I thought. The disappointments I'd had to survive were forgotten. This was it. An opening of my new play with a great star in London or New York. The prospect was thrilling. I was really going to make it big this time.

As I sat next to my hostess, I saw her exquisite face looking at me with those green, almost purple, eyes. On the wall behind her head the eyes were repeated in the famous picture by Augustus John. Sitting between us on a stool, being fed raw liver from a silver bowl was a beautiful Siamese cat, its eyes too from time to time staring at me. I felt three times hypnotized.

Sitting on my left that day in her wheelchair was the lovely Kay Hammond who had recently been struck down by a cruelly incapacitating stroke.

'If I ccccant ggget my words out, dear,' she whispered to me in her lovely voice, 'jjjust go on talking and tttake no notice.' What courage.

After lunch we all strolled in the garden before we took our leave. With more propositions about the future of my play ringing in my ears I drove off to Brighton. That visit was to be the first of many to Tickerage.

As Vivien was under moral contract to another play first for the great impresario Binkie Beaumont, my project was put back. Eager to invite Vivien to my home I cooked her one of her favourite dishes, coq au vin. As we sat enjoying our meal washed down with red wine, my budgerigar, 'Tweetie Pie', sat on Vivien's head, laughing and chatting, much to her joy. Vivien was wearing a pink costume lined with Siamese silk and dressed with scores of tiny golden brooches worn like a row of medals across her chest. With her eyes made up Cleopatra-style and that perfect face she looked, as ever, stunning. She and the two friends with her created a wonderful atmosphere in my kitchen as we ate off my scrubbed pine table. It was after dinner that it happened. Vivien was examining one of my French military regimental insignias when she dropped senseless to the floor. As she had drunk wisely I knew it was something else which had caused her collapse. Soon she recovered. But I remember her pale beautiful face wrapped in her mink coat as she waved goodbye and thanks from the passenger seat of her Rolls Royce.

I was to see a lot of Vivien in the winter that followed. We sometimes went for long walks through her small forest, before she led us guests back to tea. Theatre stars too numerous to mention appeared for meals or weekends. Once we played charades. I will never forget the great choreographer Sir Frederick Ashton acting out 'overdraft' as he tried to be a draught coming from under the door for the second syllable. Vivien stood on the settee crying with laughter. But as I observed her my heart was uneasy. She seemed to swing from high to low. When on a high her overactive mind would not let her rest until in the early hours of the morning every ash tray had been emptied and cleaned, every cushion patted back into place.

Finally she opened in Manchester in the other play she had agreed to do. In it she had to age to a woman in her eighties. The public, used to seeing her youthful and glamorous, hated it. It ran three weeks and then the tour was called off.

Back from visits to France I would contact her. She seemed evasive and strained. Finally I realized she was perhaps too ill to do my play. The strain of waiting was for me a great ordeal. But knowing her was a double ordeal, for one basked in the warmth of her friendship as one grew more anxious about her health.

One day she took me for a drive. Seated in the back of the Rolls, her mink coat and a huge box of chocolates spread on her knees, we nibbled as we journeyed. That day she told me the whole of the story of how she read *Gone with the Wind* and how she had known from the very first pages that she was going to play Scarlett O'Hara. She described some highlights from the filming of it, particularly of her private dislike of having to kiss Clark Gable.

Finally she turned to me with those famous eyes sadder than I have ever seen them. 'You know, Allon, five people have already died connected with that film.' And then she listed them. 'Clarkie, Leslie Howard, Ona Munsen, who played Belle Crystal, Margaret Mitchell and finally the producer, Selznick.'

I will never forget the look of sadness as her beautiful eyes spoke to me. Who would be the next?

Intuitively answering her question, I said, 'After all, death is not final, it's just like going through a door into the next room.'

She sat silently digesting my words.

Still waiting for any hint of a hope that she might yet get my play on the road, I was in Paris working on something else when I read the news. Vivien Leigh was ill. I hurried back to Britain as a letter from me to her went ahead. I found her reply waiting for me at Brighton. It was a postcard of Tobias the angel in mosaic. On the back she had written, 'It will only be three months . . . come and see me when you're back in London.'

I rested one day to wash shirts and prepare myself. That afternoon as I closed my flat door ready to go to the beach for a swim I had a curious experience. Lying on the stairs by my top floor flat was a black gauntlet glove. As I looked back at in wonder it vanished. Mystified, I sped to the beach and laid myself out in the sun. Being still travel weary, I slept. As I awoke maybe ten minutes later I stretched out my arms above my head as one does. My right hand touched something cold and slimy. Looking up, I saw under my hand a large motor-cyclist's gauntlet glove. It was black and paired exactly the ghost glove I'd seen on my stairs. Hating the feel of this real glove I rose up, and, running to the sea, I threw it in a great arc. It fell, splash, to disappear in the calm sea. Two minutes later, an acquaintance strolling across the sand towards me said casually, 'Just heard the news bulletin on my transistor. Vivien Leigh is dead.' I froze.

I didn't attend Vivien's funeral; the immediate family wanted it quiet. I sent a bunch of her favourite blue sweet-peas.

A short time later, my heart still heavy, I was washing up my lunch plate in my kitchen when it happened. Spinning through the wall, a living vision of beauty, was Vivien. She wore a black cocktail-type dress with a huge diamond splash of light at her neck. After a swift pirouette she stood still as she gazed at me, smiling.

'You're quite right Allon, dying was nothing, it was just like going through a door, and, being an actress, I made a wonderful entrance.' Then she was gone.

I knew in my heart she had come back to thank me for the service I had rendered her, not as a writer, but as a healer. I had helped her to go through the thing she most feared, dying. I understood in that moment she was never destined to do my play. It had merely been a method to bring about our meeting, so that I could help her. I nearly wept with shock and joy. Vivien was alive and well on another time level, and she had wanted, perfect friend that she was, to tell me. And, meticulous as ever, she had shown herself to me for the telling.

When all the theatre people gathered in St Martin's in the Fields for her memorial service I stood amongst so many famous faces as we all sang the great anthem *Glory, Glory, Alleluia*. As I walked down the steps into Trafalgar Square watching the others going off to their luncheon appointments at whatever restaurant, I went alone for a sandwich and a pint. I had lost not only my leading lady, I had lost a dear friend. And now what of the future for me? One by one in the past year possibilities of productions had closed their invisible doors on me. I was back on the outside looking in. It felt to me that my theatre-writing career had met its worst block. With heavy heart I thought, what next? Somewhere locked inside me was a curious feeling of waiting. But waiting for what? I was soon to know.

4.
THE DEVELOPING CIRCLE

EXPOSED as I was to the sometimes bewildering vicissitudes of trying to built a creative career as a writer and composer, I had sometimes consulted a lady clairvoyant. Since, during her life she never sought publicity, indeed had a horror of it, now that she is in another world I shall still respect her wishes. Suffice to say that she was a charming woman with great gifts who endlessly sought to use them to help those who consulted her. When the going got tough, I was glad to enter the calm of her room heated by the inevitable paraffin stove and decorated by an abundance of pictures of a spiritual nature and highly-coloured cushions. For a small sum she would cut the cards and read either or both hands, for a slightly larger fee she would gaze into a fairly large crystal after unwrapping it tenderly from its covering of black velvet. The information she gave was sometimes surprisingly helpful and accurate. But most of all she gave the courage to fight on. Walking the short distance back from her home to mine, I always carried a light in my heart where there had sometimes been flickering despair. One sensed she was a good woman with a strong spiritual light about her.

On the occasion of this particular visit, I was surprised by the strength of her tone as she said to me, 'We know you are a creative man with several talents which you have been working at – but what you don't seem to accept is your undoubted talents as a psychic.' The lady gazed at me to seek my reaction to this statement.

'So what do I do about it?'

'This is a God-given talent which you must not waste. You develop it – that's what.' She gazed again into my eyes, watching for my response.

'How?'

'I'll tell you exactly how. On Mondays I run a developing circle for mediumship, and on Fridays for healing. I suggest you attend both.'

I was so surprised by this sudden interest in my psychic awareness that I not only agreed but I also forgot to pay the lady as I hurriedly left; a fact we laughingly put right on our next meeting.

The following Monday I presented myself as suggested a little before eight o'clock in the evening at the terraced house where the clairvoyant lodged. On this, as on all other occasions, I was greeted at the front door by the owner of the house, a cheerful woman of imposing stature, who led me into the downstairs living room to what was to become my regular chair. Seated in a circle of about a dozen or more people I was introduced to the others. We were a motley assortment of both sexes and all ages from twenty to fifty or more.

After a pause the clairvoyant appeared, taking her place in a special chair by the mantelpiece. It was a pleasant, dimly lit room where we were gathered; there was music playing of a religious nature. I was given a rosary to conform with all the others and we were invited to pray. The clairvoyant led us in prayer with a few simple words, placing us in the Light of God for our protection before we went into silence. I sensed a great feeling of friendship and warmth as our individual selves seemed to mould into one unity.

It has to be said here that a good psychic cannot be made from the wrong material, any more than a good cricketer or a first-class cook or engineer. The flair has to be there. The exercises and meditations which we were encouraged to carry out in our circle were simply practical methods of intensifying, exercising and learning to understand our sixth senses.

On closing our eyes and relaxing in a pre-meditative manner some of us became aware of small dots of light coming towards us rather similar to separate flakes of snow which hit the windscreen of a car, or approaching specks of light. After exercise and patience these dots of light will separate and become faces. Often at first these faces may not be meaningful or recognizable, but they will finally slow down and become both. Gradually, as we further develop we realize we are working to perfect a system called mediumship, which enables us to receive our 'television' pictures from another time level beyond death.

One of the first lessons to learn in psychic development is to be able to separate the experiences of the imagination from those of the psychic senses. Only time and practice will develop this sense of being able to differentiate these two very dissimilar happenings.

The purpose of having a good teacher to lead you through early psychic experiences, is to have someone more experienced as a sensitive than yourself to help you sort out what is happening within or about you, and how to deal with it. At first you feel shy about speaking out about some of the rather bewildering phenomena which can manifest. You soon learn to share these with your group under the watchful eye of your leader. So it was with me.

I learned that the mental images and sounds of a psychic's awareness are roughly divided into two: clairvoyance, which is the use of the third eye known since ancient times, and clairaudience, which is the use of the third ear – in my case based near my physical ear over my right shoulder. The pictures I see on my third eye can be likened to a small colour television which operates in a space between the eyebrows. The sounds of clairaudience can sometimes be linked to a whisper and sometimes the dialogue seems to be born somewhere in the brain. Sometimes the communication takes the form of third-eye-visible symbols which one has to learn to interpret. At first a lot of mistakes can be made in this interpretation, but with practice skill and confidence grows.

One can, it seems, describe more fully the biological apparatus that man possesses to make him aware of his psychic or sixth sense. The third eye is indeed placed just in front of the pituitary gland. This lies inside the human skull behind the eyebrows. Another essential part of the body which functions to motivate psychic awareness is the pineal gland. This lies further into the head behind the pituitary gland on the point of axis coming down from the centre of the head.

To understand further the apparatus of man which registers his psychic senses we should also mention the hypothalamus gland. Descartes described the soul of man as lying in the hypothalamus gland. This is situated just above the pineal gland. The hypothalamus is the controlling link between the higher and lower brain. It seems it also controls our automatic nervous system by varying the production of adrenalin within our bodies.

In a properly evolving personality, spiritually aware and truly balanced, it is said that perfect balance must be obtained between the pineal gland, which in its shape represents the male organ of man, and the pituitary, which represents the female.

In making even a simplified study of man's apparatus for the use of his ESP (Extra Sensory Perception) we start to learn what a sophisticated being he is. Man was designed not only to function on a physical level but also on a spiritual one. For some reason modern man is today using only a part of his potential, which maybe he once used fully. The growing awareness of this neglect may already be leading man to learn or to re-learn to extend the use of his brain, an organ which harbours his soul as well as his mind. An an ex-medical student I marvel as I try to update my studies. As a developing psychic I marvelled also at the experiences which broke about me and within me in the weekly circle.

We sometimes had visiting mediums to our circle who each taught us something different. One of these, I remember, instructed us about the energy centres of the body – or the *chakras* as the eastern teaching names them.

The etheric body of man, inter-relating as it does with the physical, is scattered with many small energy centres and seven main ones. These seven chakras are situated in various parts of the body. They include amongst others, working from the lowest to the highest, the perenium, the spatum (that flat area just above the tail or coccyx attached to the spinal column), the solar plexus, the heart, the throat and the top of the head. When studying yoga, by a technique of deep breathing the consciousness of man is trained to linger at first in the lower or animal centres and then after progressing through many stages is finally brought up through the heart to the head chakra. Once the head chakra is opened, a double happening is put into operation. The person both gives out and receives Cosmic Energies from their fully operating head antenna. After learning and using the breathing technique over a regular period we as students achieved this state. I personally found that the opening of my head chakra brought two main experiences. I sensed a great feeling of being tuned in to new energies radiating in the Cosmic supply made further available to me, and a huge increase in my own sensitivity. I was warned that once this head chakra or sacred flame is energized one has to learn to protect oneself from other influences which might impinge on this newly-active psychic apparatus. I had to learn to close down and protect myself whilst mingling with people at random, particularly on public transport for example. All new knowledge brings added responsibility. My newly-opened head chakra was to bring me a whole new awareness of my psychic abilities, and I was fully aware of the responsibility of my growing powers.

In developing one's mediumship, a person sensitizes and practices using their receiving apparatus for wavelengths higher than the normal communication between human beings. Clairaudience receives sounds radiated on a higher level than picked up by the human ear and clairvoyance receives pictures put out on a higher vibration than that received by the human eyes. In this way, a medium or sensitive can receive communication from other time levels than the one on which we live for example on planet Earth. When a soul goes through the change of existence we call death, that soul assumes a spiritual body and existence invisible to us here, but solid and complete to those on their new vibration. That is why a medium on planet Earth can pick up signals from those we wrongly call dead. Some of these beings living a busy and multivarious life on another time level do not wish to give the time or the energy to try to communicate with us on our lower vibration of life. They perhaps are so happy to be free from the experience of having done one or more lives on planet Earth (known to some as the Vale of Tears) that they concentrate totally on their new lives.

Once I had learned the technique of raising my consciousness and opening up my head chakra, all this information and much more was made available to me from various intelligences on another time level. These helpful souls want to bring down to us some of the eternal knowledge so that we can live more fully, assume our true destiny and aspire to greater knowledge than the price of a new car or how to make love in seventeen different positions. Interesting as that knowledge might be under the limited circumstances of this time level, it is not particularly of use in furnishing our soul with the wisdom it must eventually acquire to scale the heights of future spiritual existence and service.

One of my teachers from a higher plane came to be known by my fellow students as 'Bon Soir'. Because I personally have experienced more than one previous life which was French-speaking, this particular teacher put out his thought forms in that language. In fact, as with music, thought forms are international and cross all time and space barriers. Nevertheless their source can be, as in this case, linked with a previous life where memory plays its part.

Because most of my fellow companions in the developing circle were, by being British, quite naturally unaware of the fact that *bon soir* means good evening in French, when my teacher started to talk through me to the circle using as his opening words, 'Bon soir,' they quite naturally presumed that this was his name. In that way this particular communicating spirit using me as his medium became to be known as 'Bon Soir'. I found this charming and I never let on. When one fellow sitter said to me one Monday, 'Bon Soir hasn't been through tonight,' I took it in my stride and was curiously touched by their interest.

Over the following weeks and months whether I was moved to give one of my addresses in the circle, or whether I was meditating with my newly-opened head chakra, I received many lectures on matters spiritual which I found deeply informative. There is not space here to itemize or explain fully all the inspired talks I received, but I would like to share with you enough of the material to demonstrate the sort of information which came through. Although the concepts are naturally mind-expanding to certain people, whether educated or not to think differently, the phraseology was always simple enough for the average mind to digest. Intellectuality was never allowed to be a barrier to the advancement of learning with Bon Soir.

Bon Soir spelt out for me in simple terms a lot of knowledge which tied up with previous studies I had made on theology and mysticism. As the information was fed into my receiving antenna, and given sound through my mouth, my brain was fully awake and listening with as much interest as anyone to the information thus received.

One of the earliest talks was to explain in all simplicity what was referred to as the System. Whether we believe in a God or not the System works on. Each one of us as separate unique and identifiable soul, proceeds on an endless journey of experience. It always has been thus, and always will be. Our concept of the process may vary owing to our circumstances, but the System carries on, taking every single living form with it.

It is an integral part of the System that we live many lives on many levels of time. By the nature of our consciousness each life we live seems, to most of us, the only life. Mostly we cannot remember previous lives, nor do we get anything but the smallest hint about future lives. Many religious attitudes do teach us their philosophy, and from this we gather (some of us) comfort and faith, but our minds are so constructed that we mostly cannot refer to our overall life's memory bank except at certain moments of instruction which I will refer to later. This memory cut-out is a part of the System. Without it we would retain a jumbled mass of memory experience which would overbalance our emotional reaction as well as our built-in soul reaction. We would be consciously reacting now to events in previous lives to the point that this would be intolerable to contain. Everything we think, do, speak and act upon is, however, recorded and affects our lives present, past and future, in spite of the fact we are largely unaware of this fact. For the System works by what we can refer to as the Law.

The Law knows neither mercy nor pity. It can also be seen as perfect, joy-giving, abundant and fulfilling beyond the miniscule mind of mortal man. If we look at the Law through the religious eyes of our faith of the moment, we interpret it through the vision of that faith. Some Christians believed, and still do, that Judgement Day is a time when dead souls resurrect at the sound of the awakening trumpet, and, furnished with spiritual bodies, they then line up before God to be tried. They are then sent to Hell for their sins where they suffer grievously, or they are sent to the Elysian Fields, where they meet up with their loved ones 'gone before and sit about on clouds playing harps and leading a presumably fairly useless but euphoric existence administered to, in all likelihood, by the angelic beings. So they think.

Study any religion and you will see their window on the System and their interpretation of the Law differs. As we experience life after life, so our own vision, teaching, and interpretation of the Law will also differ. Sometimes we will live lives un-influenced by any religious doctrine. Those lives whether, we like it or not, will still be in harmony with the Law. Many good people live excellent, fulfilling and creative lives with totally non-religious attitudes. Many people live partly self-destructive lives announcing their religious beliefs and making public show of them. It makes no difference. The Law still works and contains us all. What we say we do and say we think is, ultimately, not the essential. The essential is what we do think, and what we carry out. The Law is perfect and works perfectly. We are on the vibration of thought which is struck by our inner emotions. There can be no cheating for any one of us, now, then or in the future. I, as a writer and psychic, may be communicating to you my thoughts on these matters as I see them. But if in my heart I really feel differently, then it is those thoughts which register on my destiny. For, as Bon Soir explained, knowledge my soul already knew, the Law is omnipotent, perfect and ever-active. To those who live and think through the attitude of their religious faith, the Law might be interpreted as God. Whether one believes in God or not makes no difference, for He is. Whether one believes in the Law or not makes no difference either. The Law is.

The teachings of Bon Soir continued to come through me during continued visits to our developing circle. After a while those who attended started to have a picture of his attitudes concerning the System and the Law which built up piece by piece to gradually fill the picture. All the pieces seemed to fit into one another, and viewed in their entirety there seems to be no argument between one section and another. It was as if the entire teaching was already manifest on a higher plane, and that Bon Soir revealed it to us a piece at a time.

One continuous theme of this teaching was that of reincarnation. To educate our souls we have to lead many lives on many time levels. Planet Earth is but one of a vast number. Jesus's teaching, 'In my Father's house there are many mansions' is so often quoted. He was explaining to us about the System in parable form. We have to live lives as men, women, rich, poor, sick, strong. We live lives in bodies with white, black or yellow skins and all the shades between if necessary to teach us about the System. Gradually as we love, hate, conquer or be conquered, amass fortunes or lose them, suffer, rejoice, consume or be consumed, so we hopefully inch forward in our soul's education. We go from time level to time level as various lives are made available to us, lives suited to teach us this lesson or that. Whether we luxuriate in our comforts, suffer from our illnesses, die in our wars or live peacefully with our fellow man only one thing emerges of any importance. Our souls are gradually aspiring to higher knowledge as we advance to higher realms of existence. The experience is tough, rewarding, painful and joyful. Gradually we learn that our spiritual life is the only real existence, and that each mortal life is but temporal. Some of us learn apparently faster than others, but possibly some of us have elected to take the toughest routes with the biggest challenges taking us to the highest possible advances. As a result we sometimes elect to rest through possibly a fairly non-descript life whilst we gather our energies and then review the situation.

In between each life we meet with our teachers, guides and guardian angels. In their inspiring and loving presence we lick our wounds, recover from our absurdities, are thanked for our services to our brother souls and we study in the Halls of Learning. These can be looked upon as the universities of the Cosmos. The universal souls of great knowledge are constantly watching over us and creating courses for our edification and knowledge, should we desire to attend. The total artists we knew as da Vinci, Beethoven, Mozart or Raphael, to name but a few, are still manifesting and giving out their teaching of form, colour composition and quality. During our many lives and in between we are obliged to absorb all this knowledge and more if we are to advance. The task is endless and mind-expanding in its vision. We learn to use our Cosmic Energy to aspire to higher and finer planes of existence, as we choose to serve our brother man and link up with the angelic forces of the Hierarchy. The human mind can only glimpse the glory and the wonder of the System. It is the equipment given to us students as we plod on with our given and chosen tasks. But the human mind can always respond to divine and superb inspiration. Even we humans on planet Earth can be lit up at precious moments by the Cosmic Light which transforms clay to spirit. The energies are there for the using no matter how dim our vision. As we hold up our individual, tiny, cracked mirrors, we can reflect the great light of Cosmic Energy. For this permeates through every level of existence as it draws us up and onward in our endless quest for development – known to us or not. We are, we were, and we will be.

All this teaching and more came to me as I sat giving out the words of Bon Soir in the developing circle. It was also revealed to me, with much more, as my soul memory was awakened by my newly-formed discipline of meditation heightened by the opening of my head chakra.

I was aware that I could have let myself be completely over-shadowed by certain visiting personalities from other time levels, should I have agreed. But my curiosity as a human being always prevented this. I have never wanted to drink too much at parties because the following day you cannot remember what happened; as a writer I like to remember. (The damage to one's body also offends me.) In the same way, trance work, by its very nature, removes you from the scene of consciousness. To be over-shadowed or deeply inspired by a visiting personality is quite another thing. Naturally these visitors have to be vetted, examined and only allowed near if they are of sufficient merit to allow them into your private universe. We all have guardian angels whose duty extends to watching carefully who approaches us whilst we are in a state of raised consciousness. Once we have established a working basis with our gate-keeper, no way can the wrong influences approach us. They are kept very much at bay, to vanish once we have placed our work in the Light. Have no fear of them.

Concerning these spiritual links, it has been suggested that our so called spiritual 'guides' are in fact another part of ourselves, possibly a higher part. If this is so I would have thought it would have been revealed to us. Naturally, as a medium I am fascinated by what I experience. On the other hand endless introspection into psychic workings can be unwise. Better use the energy in the work itself.

If, on the other hand, our 'guides' are simply manifestations of images formed in our over selves (the highest part of our being) which are bringing knowledge down to our lower selves, provided what they teach us is edifying and constructive, where is the problem? All religions have their own God. He can be seen in many different ways. The other point which struck me so strongly from the teachings of Bon Soir was that all the religious and the scientific attitudes to the great mysteries, once followed through, lead to the same knowledge. He explained that there is no war between science and religion. It is a matter of being broad-minded enough to examine each attitude long enough and deeply enough to find out that they lead to the same truths. The picture varies with the observer, but the picture is the same. The Cosmos is there, only man interprets it differently.

Another area of interest to me was the information Bon Soir brought through about time-space knowledge. Because we are at the moment living lives on planet Earth nearing the end of the twentieth century, our conception of time is for the most part limited by our circumstances. Time is in fact an illusion. We think from our viewpoint that time is a piece of string starting way behind us and carrying us through the knot we call 'now' to the knot we call 'death' and then on to the future. In fact there are many levels of time co-existing in a manner probably impossible to contain in mortal mind as it now operates. Some advanced scientists, philosophers, etc, including, of course, the visionary Einstein, can contain in their mortal consciousness a much greater vision of time. To try to simplify the vision of time as explained to me, let us stand on a clear night with a reasonably efficient telescope available to the average person. Look at the furthest star you can glimpse. Realize now that the light travelling from that star to your eye has already taken possibly seven hundred years. We, watching, are surrounded by twentieth-century happenings. The star you are looking at is witnessing the time of the crusades. That knowledge must alter the average man's aspect of time. Multiply that knowledge by the number of the other planets, some as yet unknown to us, and you get a rough idea of the immensity of the subject.

One aspect of time which Bon Soir referred to was also of great fascination to me. He told me that man would one day discover a means of journeying through space (and so through time) which would make the present rocket-fired space vehicles as old-fashioned as the horse and cart. When this occurs an enormous break-through will take place in man's understanding of time-space knowledge. For he will be able to journey through his own time of death into a level of time he can only reach at present by dying. At this moment religion and science will finally link up. The heavenly spheres will be attainable through package holidays. If this sounds stupid, put it another way. Man will accept as natural a journey into the realms of heaven which at present he has to die to experience.

Another of Bon Soir's talks was about the important meetings with our guides and our guardian angels when we review after 'death' the life we have just finished and plan of our next life. He likened it to breakfast with one's professor at university to discuss our studies and the exams to come, or being sent for by our manager in a business when our progress, future, weaknesses and failures might be discussed.

The idea of this meeting must be awe-inspiring. Whenever I meditate on the subject, I am always shown the setting which 'Bon Soir' described to us one evening in such simple terms:

> You must picture a round table where you will be surrounded on each side by your teachers and guides. You will not attend this meeting until you are fully rested and recovered from your recent 'death'. You come to the meeting voluntarily when you feel ready. In the centre of the table is a globule of light and movement you could liken to television in the round. In this globule, you can see at will any moment of your previous life or if you so wish, lives. It is an awesome experience which takes courage. There will be moments of great joy, and of great sorrow. You will understand, my brother, the full awareness of the phrase from higher teaching, 'Judgement Day is now.'
>
> You will probably be not capable of assimilating and dealing with all the emotions which will course through you during this résumé of your soul's experience, so you will need the full support of your guides and helpers. There are many times you may have to break away from the viewing, and be taken to your area of repose before you are ready to continue. Imagine the torment of a mass murderer or a leader of men into evil wars designed for selfish gain and power. To contemplate the average man's short-comings is enough, wrong thoughts, opportunities to help our brother man neglected. But imagine also the joy re-lived of sharing love and companionship with friends and partners. All is re-lived. All experience is now fully understood as tests. The responsibility of guiding your own life and the influence of those about you is, perhaps for the first time, fully understood. The words of a great teacher, Jesus, are revealed in all their value. 'You must love one another, and only do to one another what you would wish they do unto you.' The Law is thus truly revealed and understood.

To complete the picture concerning reincarnation which Bon Soir drew for us, he explained the process of choosing a future life after the rest and re-education period is over. Should we so desire it, having realized the necessity of continuing with our soul education, we possibly choose to come back to planet Earth for another life here. It is then decided what the main features of the life are to be. If we have badly handled a previous rich life we might choose a poor one. If we have wasted power and glory, we may need struggle and poverty to teach us. Or vice versa. All must be experienced. Similarly the right background and family is chosen for us to provide the experiences we need. When finally the moment for our re-birth arrives, we are sent off on the adventure with the best wishes of our guides and teachers. Our guardian angel, the one who has chosen to devote time which could otherwise be spent perhaps more selfishly, promises us his support from the moment of re-birth to the moment of our next 'death'. So we inherit two main influences in our new life, the chromosomes of our physically-linked forebears, and the experiences of our soul. If we are sufficiently advanced we will be aware of the third and greatest influence, that available to us through prayer and meditation by linking with our guides and teachers and the angelic forces about us on higher vibrations. They will always supply us with power and inspiration provided we do the work to make this possible. Such is the System. Such is the Law. And one day it will not be necessary for us to return to such basic experiences as a life on planet Earth. For we will finally have merited an advance to higher realms.

All this and more came through the teaching of Bon Soir who first came to me all those years ago in the intimacy of our developing circle on those Monday nights in Brighton.

One of the early evidential pieces of information which I was allowed to bring through from another time level during my early meditations in our circle concerned the film star Nigel Green. That particular Monday, after we had opened as usual with prayers and then gone into the silence, quite suddenly the huge spirit form of Nigel appeared in the middle of our group. He looked well and full of dynamic energy which seemed to make him insist on being noticed. With his frame, six foot and over, moving about in front of me, how could I not see him – spirit though he was. For Nigel had been dead already some few weeks.

Normally when I see pictures transmitted from another time level, as I have explained, I see them on the small colour television screen we call the third eye. This is known as objective clairvoyance. Occasionally, as with my mother, the re-appearance of Vivien Leigh, and now Nigel, the vision is seen apart from me externally. This is known as subjective clairvoyance. When this occurs the figures are life-size. They nearly always have a curious opalescent and part transparent quality about them, bathed as they are in a special light.

On this occasion I saw Nigel subjectively. He was in a state of certain excitement when he realized that I could see him, and that he could manifest. Pacing about in his usual manner, he was drawing my attention to a large board hanging on the wall halfway down the left-hand side of the room we occupied. The board was framed, of a large size, and covered with green baize. On it, three quarters of the way up, a handsome crucifix about nine inches high was fixed. The rest of the board was used for notices, concerning, if I remember rightly, our absent healing patients. Nigel kept approaching the board and touching it as he excitedly turned his head towards me, saying to my third ear, 'I gave this, tell them I gave them this.' He nodded his head as he smiled with the pleasure the visit and the knowledge he was imparting was giving him.

I waited impatiently in silence as we sat out the rest of the meditation, when it was customary to share with the group and our teacher any experiences which had occurred.

I had known Nigel and his wife, Pamela, before he became internationally famous as a film actor. Together with their robust young daughter, they made an attractive family.

Nigel, as with everyone in the theatre, had to live through many vicissitudes. He had made a good reputation as a young man acting Shakespeare. He seemed a restless spirit with enormous energy, sometimes misplaced. A deep-thinking man, after much soul-searching he converted to Catholicism, which for a while seemed to bring him a certain comfort. It was no secret to his friends that he lived through terrible bouts of depression whilst out of work, which sometimes led to a glass too many of the hard stuff. A tremendously likeable fellow, he caused all his friends both anxious and heart-warming moments when we came across him in his cups. He shared his hilariously funny stories or his deep problems openly and dramatically; thus his huge frame and personality gave out his changing moods in no uncertain terms. Dealing with him in public was sometimes a challenge.

I admired Nigel for his courage. Out of work at one time in Brighton, rather than continually having to draw the dole to support his little family, he signed on with a road gang and worked with a pick-axe and shovel repairing the highways. In winter that takes some doing. Of course he told hilarious stories about the mostly Irish fellow workers and their special sense of humour. Then came, almost out of the blue, his role in *Zulu* with Michael Caine, which immediately made Nigel a star. From then on, it was film after film. But being Nigel, the fame rested sometimes uncomfortably on him, and caused those wide shoulders to buck and heave like a stallion who resents being broken in, with a bit in his mouth and a saddle on his back. Nigel bought himself a beautiful mock tudor house with a lovely garden not even a mile from where I lived. It was his pride and joy. But as so often happens in our lives, we arrive at one goal, only to lose another even more precious. His marriage had foundered and he had to leave Pamela in the big house.

The last time I saw Nigel alive was in the local launderette. Having just spent a day filming with Richard Harris and Peter O'Toole, two of the other great trail blazers, and imbibing well on the Brighton Belle train bringing him back, Nigel was in great spirits. Much to the amazement of a quiet local lady planning a quiet half-hour tending her family's washing, on meeting me Nigel launched into his recitation of the day's events. Leaping from place to place in the launderette, and at one time even standing up on one of the machines, he gave a blow-by-blow account, taking off the other two stars in turn. It was hilarious to watch his antics and the totally bemused lady who had never experienced anything like it in her life. When another friend turned up, similarly lubricated, to join the party, I grabbed my newly-washed bed-linen and fled. I re-live the memory with joy.

Not very long afterwards, Nigel, finding the stress of his life over-burdening him, was found dead in the hallway of his apartment. He was apparently trying to ring for help, having, it seems, mixed medication with alcohol unwisely. With many other show business friends I attended his funeral. I saw Nigel present, striding about unseen by everyone else, complaining to me about the boredom of the pre-cremation service.

'I organized a beautiful service myself only a month ago,' his spirit form told me. 'And now it's mine – it's dreadful.'

When, having seen Nigel appear in the development circle, I told my teacher what I had seen, she accepted it without a murmur. Unknown to me Nigel had several times sat with the circle in question, and given the board and the crucifix as his blessing. Thank you, Nigel, for appearing so clearly to me that evening, and giving me that evidence. The event was proof to me that my powers were developing accurately, and it gave me enormous confidence and energy to continue. Nigel does ocasionally still contact me and I am happy to report that he has fully recovered from the frustration of his accidental death, and is winging his way with all his special energy towards new realms of discovery and expression for his talents.

Having given you a good idea of what transpired in our developing circle on Mondays, this is the moment to talk about our Friday meetings. The purpose of these was to give, receive and develop latent healing powers.

The room was arranged differently, to accomodate the varying number of people who were our patients. The healers were paired off as they set about their work. Because the subject of spiritual healing touched those of clairvoyance and other manifestations of mental mediumship much of what took place on Fridays would be discussed on Mondays. The two subjects were complementary. I will give an example.

Over a long period of meditation, I made contact with and became closely linked on a spiritual level with a North American Indian I learned to call Brave Spirit. He was a huge, handsome fellow of enormous presence and energy. He arrived suddenly in a vision on a beautiful black horse, dismounted and, having greeted me courteously, proceeded to show me around, as it were, his previous life. Dressed simply in a breech clout of leather, his bare torso was decorated simply with a single red feather representing the sacred flame of the head chakra which was fixed to the back of his head. Sometimes he would walk me about his herb garden explaining the cultivation of herbs and corn for food or for beneficial health-giving remedies. Helping me to climb up onto his horse, he sat me behind him and we visited the plains and valleys about his territory. We saw the quarters where the women and young children lived separately and the separate accommodation for the young men who had reached puberty and were beginning their tests of manhood. They were instructed in hunting and tested by cold and fatigue, all to prepare them for the ceremony of accepting their place in the tribe as fighting Braves, ready to die for their cause. Brave Spirit also told me about the spiritual disciplines and tribal knowledge he taught as their head, their priest, and their medicine man. They learned the importance of the liaison between man mortal and man spiritual and the linking of us here with spiritual identities on a higher plane. Each Brave worked to have one superb clear vision of a spiritual nature linking him with his etheric counterpart. Thus they understood the land of the hereafter to which they would go after death. In this way they were ready to die fighting bravely for their tribe's survival, if need be, and their place in the valley of beyond was assured. The ideals of physical perfection, bravery and spiritual knowledge were thus imprinted on the young Braves' minds, spirits and bodies as they prepared to progress through death. There was no morbid death wish, merely a goal to achieve if death in battle occurred. Their God, the Great White Spirit, who lived in and was the all-pervading Sun, lit up their lives and their spirits providing the energy to grow their crops, the rain to water them and the overall mystical presence to inspire their spiritual links. Death to them was a release to greater movement and higher expression. They revered the process of dying, rather than fearing it. They knew too, that one day they in turn would link in spirit with man on earth. Brave Spirit explained all this and more to me as he showed me around his life geographically and spiritually.

When it came to being shown the great mountain where Brave Spirit went sometimes to retreat and pray, I was allowed only to approach the valley, where I was left with his tethered horse as he climbed forward and scaled the mountain. There he would link with the Great God of the Sky as he worshipped and communed with the Great White Spirit. When he returned his whole being was charged with etheric energy, ready to give out in healing to his fellow man. So he taught me to link with the Divine Energy of God and to raise my hands up in prayer as my etheric body was charged also with the great energy capable of achieving so much.

In this way Monday's meditations were sometimes linked with Friday's healing sessions. Many other spirit influences, doctors, angelic forms and guides also manifested as they linked from their higher planes to teach us to demonstrate and use the healing energies.

Our teacher in the circle, a healer herself, taught us the simplicity of raising our consciousness in prayer and then asking that our spiritual selves be charged with the healing energies. Thus by the simple gesture of laying our hands on the patient before us, we shared this energy with them as we asked that it help them to step out of the disharmony of disease.

It was to be a whole year of studying, watching and linking in prayer with the healers working about me in that room, before one Friday I was suddenly summoned to step forward, and partnered by another of our group, to give healing. The moment I had been preparing and praying for had at last arrived. I realized the importance of this moment for me; and as if to confirm this, an experience followed which is engraved on my memory forever.

I was given as a healing partner a charming woman of uncertain age who stood the far side of the solid table by the window. We helped our patient, a woman suffering from a back problem, up onto the table via a chair used as a step. We then helped her lie down between us on a thick eiderdown which made a comfortable surface on the table. After a moment of prayer and silence my co-healer and I stretched out our hands over the patient as we gave her healing.

Then something extraordinary took place.

The rest of the room filled with people faded from my consciousness. I was suddenly transported to another level of awareness. Suddenly I was standing in a similar position with my arms outstretched over a patient, my partner similarly placed. Around and above me was a temple-like building apparently made of light. The table on which our patient lay appeared to be made of a solid crystal-like substance resembling solid light. The colours about us were crystal blue and white. Dressed in opalescent but simple robes, we stretched out our arms in the healing gesture. I was aware of a great number of other healers working about me in what I can only describe as a healing Temple of Light. The colours about us seemed to emanate from the building itself, as the feeling of peace was awe-inspiring. I knew I was translated to another time-space level. The experience lasted perhaps a minute, perhaps much longer. I could not tell. Time stood still as I was totally absorbed in the task at hand. A while later the vision about me faded and I was back standing beside our patient on the table.

I knew without a shadow of doubt that this experience had been given me to demonstrate the link between man and spirit. I had been allowed to glimpse the healing work taking place on a higher vibration, to link with the spiritual realms of Light. I knew that after a year of waiting and praying in that healing circle my work and patience had been purposeful. I knew that the heavenly and angelic forces had allowed me to experience this happening to assure me I was giving my time energy to a spiritual purpose which was already being fulfilled. I knew the path I had trod was the right one. Humbled and moved by the experience, I went home that night to my wooden house on the hill to await further development of my healing powers. The next stage of my healing story was to unfold almost immediately.

5.
THE HEALING
OF NELLIE QUINLIVAN

To strengthen even more my only recently acquired physique, I had joined a weight-training club. It was a modest and friendly club, housed in the basement of a local school. Twice a week, on my free evenings not taken up by the meditation or healing circle, I went along to join the other men and lads in humping and heaving weights. They were a friendly lot, mostly of simple backgrounds, with the natural comradeship of such folk. As they knew nothing about my image as a writer composer, or as a developing psychic and healer, I was treated as a fellow weight-trainer. I enjoyed their simplicity, and their innate good manners. My body responded well to the exercises. I was soon bench-pressing two hundred pounds, a feat I would have liked to have shown to the doctors in the sanatorium. I could never stop being grateful for the new man inside of whom I was now prospering. To prevent my new physique from becoming over-musclebound, I worked out a plan of exercises combining floor work and calisthenics with weight-lifting. I was thus faithful to the exercises I had learned in France, and to my recently-discovered enjoyment of training with weights. The post work-out euphoria I discovered balanced well with the heights of meditation and made a superb contrast to career anxieties. I thus became a much more balanced human being with a newly-developed happy-go-lucky side – so badly needed by us all to survive. I brought forth from my inner world a newly-acquired extrovert side which was to be of immense value to me as a healer. The confidence gained with my improved appearance gave me the pass key to meeting new people and fresh situations. As I mastered safely the handling of heavy weights, I also helped train several newcomers who had to learn the ropes. Surprisingly, it was this background which was to produce a startling opportunity for my healing talent.

The club was run by a huge, friendly man, a fireman by profession, by the name of Jack Quinlivan. On this particular evening, in place of the usual benevolent smile of greeting on Jack's face, I found a new expression of intense worry.

'Allon, my friend, I'm worried stiff.' He took me aside to whisper in my ear.

'What is it, Jack?'

'My wife. She's dying.'

At this I found myself replying, 'Who said so?'

'The doctors at the hospital say so.'

Again the reply seemed to come from my mouth without my bidding. 'Doctors don't always know.'

Even as I said it, a part of my brain realized what an unwise thing it would be for me to give Jack false hope. And yet some power seemed to rise up within me, filling me with confidence. I knew I had obeyed the dictates of some inner voice, something stronger than myself.

'After I've finished training, would you like me to go and see her?' Again the words tripped out.

What amazed me was Jack's reaction. His face broke into a huge smile as if I had just bestowed upon him some wonderful gift. He held my arm tightly as he replied, 'Allon, you wouldn't, would you?'

I was touched and even amazed at his positive reaction to my offer, almost as if he sensed some forthcoming event about which I was as yet not fully informed. I had never uttered one single word to Jack or any of the lads about my psychic healing activities, and yet his innocent confidence in me touched me deeply. It was as if he already knew the outcome of the story, whereas all I sensed was this force within me compelling me to play my part in the drama.

I sped away into my training clothes, worked through my exercises, washed in the primitive shower, and, dressed in my jeans and sweater, followed Jack's van in my white sports car to Hove General Hospital.

We found Jack's wife, Nellie, lying inert in a bed half way down a huge ward containing only women. As Jack led me to his wife he stood aside, leaving me alone with her. I saw lying there a tall woman, past middle age, with straight greying black hair scraped back from her forehead. She was connected by a tube to a drip machine, as oxygen was also being fed by another tube to her nose. The colour of her skin was grey yellow, under her closed eyes were wide, dark brown, almost purple, shadows which spoke to me of kidney failure. As she lay on her back, breathing heavily, she appeared to be comatose.

As I sat on the small chair by Nellie's prostrate form, I stared long and hard, taking in every detail of her. I remembered Jack telling me about the doctor's opinion. I remembered too my automatic reply. I thought as I gazed at the tired face of this woman supposedly dying, that I had been brought to her for a purpose. As I raised my consciousness with a few deep breaths, I asked that I might be used as a medium for the healing power which could save her.

As I reached out and gently held the little finger of Nellie's still hand, something extraordinary happened. On the grey cheeks of the dying woman there appeared, clearly visible, two areas of pink. As if life was gently flowing back into her weak body, the pink area gradually spread to change her corpse-like face into that of a sleeping woman. Her eyelids fluttered open, as her eyeballs, first showing only yellow white, turned down to look at me.

Still holding her finger I found myself saying, 'Hello, Nellie, you look very cheeky.'

At these seemingly inappropriate words Nellie gave a beautiful quiet smile. As her eyes focused on my face, previously unknown to her, she glanced across to Jack who nodded assurance. She gazed back at my face in quiet acceptance before she sank back, this time into sleep. I will always remember the smile which was still on her lips.

I turned to see Jack's almost incredulous face as I led him quietly away. 'Never seen anything like it,' he was muttering in suppressed excitement.

Once outside the ward he hugged me in gratitude. 'There's hope – my lovely Nellie.' Tears of bewilderment and joy poured down Jack's manly face as he gave way to the emotion surging up within him.

The next day I called to see Nellie again. I found her sitting up. I stayed but a few minutes, to give her healing and to leave without tiring her. Each time I visited I stayed a little longer. Perhaps four visits in all. Within a short while she was off the drips. Within a month she was home. Within three months she was back again in hospital to have the operation for which she was previously too ill to survive. They removed a part of a diseased kidney. Within six months she was touring Scotland with Jack in his van, living in it. It was later that Jack told me her trouble had been cancer.

Nellie was to live another ten years. I swore Jack to secrecy about the miracle we had witnessed. In the hospital the nurses referred to her as the miracle lady. Although we all knew something wonderful had taken place, I was not yet ready to go public on it. I wanted more time to absorb the happening. I did not want my colleagues in the theatre world to think I was using my new-found powers as a publicity stunt for my next production. The whole event had been of such intense value that I wanted time to absorb it, to realize the possibilities of change which it brought into my world.

I had been working through many experiences, and through many prayer hours to attune the healing powers I knew God had given me to share with my fellow man. Now that it was beginning to manifest, I knew my life could never be quite the same. So it was to prove.

6.
THE MESSENGER FROM SPIRIT

I NOTE that often in life changes without are triggered by changes within. So it was at this time for me.

I knew the lease of my flat in Brighton was coming to a close and that the rent would increase greatly should I wish to re-negotiate it. Such was the climate of the times. Anyway, I felt I had been paying enough with nothing at the end to show for it. I wanted to own a dwelling and to put down some roots. Another flat did not appeal to me, as I needed soil about me to cultivate flowers and vegetables, and the ordinary brick houses I saw for sale were either far beyond my means or boring.

At one time I seriously considered buying a house-boat, but after investigating the nearby harbours of Shoreham and Newhaven I was put off the idea by the congestion of craft already there. But a home built of wood appealed to me. As it happened I was to find my wooden dwelling set in enough ground to cultivate at my will at a price I could afford. It happened with apparent ease.

After a week of considering this idea or that, my date for decision on my lease was approaching. I tried to keep calm despite the uncertainty before me. Then, one morning early that summer, I awoke startled to see a form standing at the end of my bed. I knew that he came from another time level. Having recovered from the slight shock of wakening thus, I studied my visitor. I saw a tall, bearded figure who struck me, with his bearing and calm presence, as part soldier, part priest. His body showed the strength of a fighter, his bearded face the calm of meditation. He wore a chain-mail upper garment under a loose, linen, sleeveless over-garment. On this, across his chest, was emblazoned a huge cross. His hair was cropped to frame his face, and served to intensify the expression of strength in his eyes. As I looked he turned, and with a single gesture he pointed a strong hand away from me, along the direction of the coast road running west to east below and alongside my flat. Continuing to point along the coast, he faded. The message was clear and simple. I was to search in that direction. I rose, washed, made my simple breakfast and dressed.

After a typical day of tapping at my typewriter on some creative work, telephoning my literary agent for any news and cooking a simple meal, it was late evening before I jumped into my open sports car and headed off down the coast obeying the Messenger's command.

The cooling air refreshed me as I spun along the coast road, the green carpet of the downs unrolling over my left shoulder. I instinctively turned inland down the narrow road which leads to the village of Ovingdean. A farm and its out-dwellings clustered round the flint-walled Norman church which I had sometimes visited. Opposite stood Ovingdean Grange, from which two Frenchmen had plotted the escape from England of young Charles Stuart, son of Charles I, from the nearby harbour of Shoreham, the other side of Brighton. I thought of my soul links with France as I steered my car up the narrow hill of the small village folded in a green valley nestling on the edge of the vast South Downs. On reaching the top of the hill, I glimpsed to my right a friendly-looking horse gazing at me over a low fence. Stopping the car, I jumped out to speak to the fine animal. As I approached he gave me an almost human smile. Remembering that I kept peppermints in my car for just such a moment, I gave him one from the flat of my hand. He took it, chewed it noisily and smiled again. Then he shook his head sideways several times. Almost as if to obey the horse I put my forehead against his and turned in unison. Then I saw it.

A few yards down the lane to my right, just visible over tall grass, was the lichen-covered roof of a single-floor dwelling. Patting the horse farewell, I wandered down the hill to examine the house. I found a path leading up to an old country gate with a sign green with age saying 'Fairways'. Pushing open the oak gate I found a brick-edged path overgrown with high grass, stinging nettles and wild flowers. As I wandered up the narrow path, the dwelling ahead became clearer. Settled on a base of red brick with several steps leading up to it was a wooden house. Clinker-built like a boat, the peeling paint part-hidden by the wilderness about it spoke of recent neglect. It was wide and friendly-looking, snuggled on the edge of the downs. Here surely was the place I had in mind, a wooden house with enough ground to cultivate vegetables and flowers. As I gazed around, I saw, almost hidden by the tall grasses, a sign saying 'For Sale'.

Wandering round the back of the bungalow, I counted the many windows looking out onto a neglected rockery. Honeysuckle and pillar roses grew in profusion about a half-collapsed verandah; the scent of the honeysuckle filling the evening air with its heavy sweetness. From a vantage point at the back I could just glimpse the distant sea, another necessity I had in mind for any future home. Gazing upwards, I noticed two sets of low chimney-stacks holding two chimneys in each, with brickwork needing repointing, and a metal guttering also in need of repair. A brick watertank graced the side of the rockery.

With a feeling that I had been led to find treasure, I noted the name of the agent on the board just visible in the fading light. A few minutes later I wandered back up to my car, and, waving to the nodding horse, I made my way back down the hill and turned right onto the coast road back to Brighton.

The following morning, first thing, I rang the house agent for the price of 'Fairways'. Because it was timber-framed and clad and fifty years old, a mortgage was out of the question. But for similar reasons, as well as its remoteness, the price was low and within my means. Rejoicing, I set off back to take another look. I noticed a new road had been partly cut through the chalk bank at the back of the ample ground on which the dwelling stood.

Asking a workman on the site of a new house being built nearby he told me in his Sussex accent, 'The lady what owns the place lives down below, mate.'

He pointed towards the church and the village. Striding down the steep hill below 'Fairways' I came across a young lad kicking a ball on the grass bank.

'You want Mrs Halliday,' he told me with a shy smile.

I noticed his regular features, his country-bred stalwart build topped by a head of corn-coloured hair.

He added, happily, 'My name's Paul, I was born at 'Fairways'. We live here now in our house which my Dad built.' He pointed proudly at the handsome red brick house perched on the bank above him. Thanking him, I walked on down into the village, knowing I was being guided at every step.

'I want 'Fairways' to go to the right owner. My father acquired it as a summer home for all of us family. I spent a great deal of my youth there.'

Mrs Halliday was speaking in her living room, having answered the door to me a while before. I noticed her almost psychic gaze. This woman with a kindly, ageing face was interviewing me, enquiring as to my worthiness to buy 'Fairways'. As I explained that I was a writer she seemed to understand my seeking a quiet place to work. As I thought too about my healing activities, almost as if in reply to my unspoken idea, Mrs Halliday added, 'It is a curious thing, but all my friends who stayed there got better.'

I knew already the soil on which 'Fairways' was built had good positive vibrations. I had already learned the value of using unseen good vibrations, known as good telluric energies, as a background for prayer work. I sensed instinctively I had been led to the right setting for my development as a healer.

'I write music also,' I added. 'My piano is this wide.' I produced a knotted piece of string from my pocket, carefully measured for the purpose.

I sensed I had passed my examination as a suitable owner of 'Fairways' as Mrs Halliday said, after producing a large black key from her writing desk, 'Take this. You have my permission to explore the house inside and out for as long as you care. Visit in the day, visit in the night. I want you to be certain you will be happy there should you still wish to buy it.' Thanking her, I left.

Anxious to enter the wooden house, I climbed back up the steep hill, and entering once more the overgrown garden, I walked up the red-brick steps to the front door and turning the black key, let myself in. Passing through a glassed-in loggia ideal for plants, I opened a second half-glazed door into the main area of the house. I found myself in a square room which served as a large connecting area between a kitchen and a bathroom off to the right, and a snuggery off to the left. Beyond the snuggery I found a narrow corridor running transversely and leading to three rooms. One I decided would be my bedroom, one room at the back would be a work room and the smaller middle room could be for the odd guest. I had counted seven rooms, the mystical number which crops up so often in my life. My present telephone number ended with 347, my car number plate carried the figures 347 and I was living in a house containing my flat and numbered 7. The omens seemed favourable. I examined the fireplace in the snuggery backing onto a similar one in the central room and noticed the wooden ceilings sloping up to a central dividing line and strengthened with wide beams running crossways a foot above my head. In spite of the peeling white paint outside, the house was as dry as a water-tight craft. I realized I was lucky to have had a builder live in the house before. Apart from a few repairs needed to the verandah which graced the back of the central part of the house, the main structure seemed sound. As I jumped on the floor the wood sprung back like a well-laid deck.

Having gazed out of every window I wandered into the small kitchen. A solid-fuel boiler for heating the water filled a stone inset to the left; to the right was a large bay window with a wide shelf. I sat on the shelf and stared out at the superb view. My eyes travelled across the overgrown garden, past the wooden fence and beyond to the sweep of the immense green valley. Part of the hill leading up to the skyline was cultivated with rich green corn. Other sections held cows grazing like toys placed at random. An old flint wall ran away and up into the distance as it divided farmland from the flint-walled church partly visible beyond a group of cottages trimmed with old trees. The peace of this edge of the downland was impressive. Scudding clouds traced their speeding shadows across the valley. I felt at peace.

Taking the string from my pocket I measured the space in the central room beside the front door. My piano would fit to the nearest inch. I opened the half-glass door at the back opposite the front door. The house was light and yet cosy. I knew I could work with the back door open onto the wild garden. Closing the door I traced my steps back to the kitchen to gaze again at the hypnotic view.

I cannot tell how long I had been staring into the valley, my mind releasing itself from the immediate problems, before the vision of the Messenger appeared. Whereas before he had startled me by his proximity, this time, as if to comply with my unspoken request, he appeared further away. His tall figure was standing in a clearing surrounded by wild grass below and a few feet away from the window where I sat. This time he stood against a great cross of light echoed in form by the tall cross-handled sword against which he was gently leaning. His eyes, staring at me calmly from his neatly-trimmed bearded face, seemed to gaze into my soul. Again I noticed the cross which adorned the shirt-like garment held to his waist by a belt. This time a cloak fell about his shoulders, opening to frame the authority of his noble presence. Whereas my mind had been centred on the problems of money for buying the house, its remoteness and the change of lifestyle that would bring, the calm within me was now fortified by this presence. I was reminded of the words, 'Be still and know.'

Then, in spite of the window between us, I seemed to hear the following words fall into my mind, as if spoken by the commanding presence before me, 'Here you will lay down your cloak for a while. Here you will receive and bring comfort to the sick and the troubled.'

As if to dramatize his words, the Messenger moved his cloak about him, indicating the land on which he stood. Then, with a final lifting of his head, he held his sword closely to him before gathering his cloak about him and vanishing.

So I knew that the buying of 'Fairways' was not just the acquisition of a future home, but more. It was to be the place where my healing powers would manifest further. Whatever the difficulties and the tasks ahead, I knew I must tackle them. A new and wider experience was awaiting me there.

When I showed my home to be to a girlfriend, she was fascinated by the place and offered kindly to make the curtains. After lots of measuring, further talks with Mrs Halliday concerning the septic tank, heating problems and so on, I made my offer in writing to the agent and was accepted. I knew that an enormous amount of physical work lay ahead of me to restore the wooden house to life. What I did not know was the full implication of the Messenger's words. The sick and troubled were indeed to find me. I was yet to have to accept the wonders which were to unfold. Too sudden a realization might have burnt me out. I was being prepared in stages for the healing work I was to be inspired to carry out. As a human vessel, my cup was indeed destined to be full and brimming over. Meanwhile I had to roll up my sleeves and attack the preparatory work for my new home.

As the authorities decreed, I had to completely re-wire my wooden house. Fortunately one of my colleagues at the gym was a qualified electrician, so he undertook the task with me as assistant. There was plenty of space under the house which I got to know well, as, wriggling on my back, I learned to push and pull the new wiring through holes in the floor and skirting boards which we drilled for the purpose. To combat any wood-worm we also, faces masked, sprayed the timbers with the appropriate chemicals. I was glad when both those laborious tasks were completed. Having installed wall lights and some modified oil-lamps hanging from the beams, we celebrated one summer night sitting in the long grass with a bottle of beer gazing back at the little house with all its windows lit.

As the walls inside were newly-painted white, I acquired a large drum of sand-coloured flat-wall paint and, using that as a background, added some Italian red for the snuggery with one wall papered in a near William Morris design of yellow and red. I stripped the linoleum off the centre room floor and, after sanding the tongued and grooved planks, I varnished them to a golden shine. The black piano and some rugs furnished the space. Having filled the walls with my own pictures, framed mostly in silver with wide black mounts, I searched the street markets for then bottom-priced Victorian and Edwardian bamboo furniture which looked perfect in its new setting. I bought a bale of plain, heavy, linen, yellow cloth for the curtains and they were made as promised by a woman friend, each pair with wide bands of the same material to dress them during the day. Having been given two huge, tall backed, easy chairs for the snuggery by a dealer who had thrown them out, I bought two turquoise stretch covers, which blended with the fitted turquoise carpet in this section of my house. The effect at night with the fire lit and the oil lamps switched on was like being on a ship riding high on the Sussex Downs. The Messenger had done me proud. The peace and the colour about me was the setting I needed. After much difficulty I acquired a telephone wired to me from some distant pole.

'Bit lonely up 'ere, ain't it, mate?' the smiling weather-beaten face of the engineer enquired anxiously. 'Better off now you're in touch with the rest of us.' With that he closed the door and strode away.

The remoteness of my house was indeed a challenge I had to face, but now I had my telephone as well as my head chakra for receiving and transmitting messages.

If I had been, because of my contacts with the theatre world,

Lance Corporal Allon Bacon, Home Guard and Officers Training Corps, Rugby School.

My Mother, née Lewis Bacon.

My Father as a Subaltern in the Cheshire Regiment 1914, later to become Sir Roger Sewell Bacon KG., M.B.E.

My Grandmother, Charlotte Bacon.

My Great Aunt, Lady Marie Hall.

My first publicity photo as actor. *(Photo Edmund Harrington)*

Vivien Leigh at Tickeridge. *(Photo by the Author)*

'Brave Spirit' original acrylic on board 24"×26". *(Black and white reproduction of painting by the Author)*

Opposite: Publicity photo for launching my second musical. *(Photo David McEnery)*

Myself at 'Fairways'.

on the cocktail invitation circuit in Brighton, now distance made me just that more unavailable. In the eyes of many I had already dropped out. Some even referred to me as the new hermit on the hill. They did not understand the changes in my life which had brought this about. How could they? I had not discussed my prayer life with any except a few most intimate friends. One of my friends who tracked me down by taxi, bearing her and a huge jeroboam bottle of champagne, was the actress Hermione Baddeley.

Hermione, known to her friends as 'Totie', had already lived a large part of her extraordinary life and career when I had met her. She became a star at eighteen when Noël Coward had, recognizing her talent, written *Poor Little Rich Girl* for her, one of his timeless hit songs placed in a revue. He wrote this particular song about her because Hermione had already married David Tennent, one of the wealthiest men of his generation.

As she told me herself, 'I had achieved everything at eighteen.' Then she smiled, pausing in her unique manner before adding quietly, 'All I had to do was to go backwards.'

We laughed together as we did on countless occasions, sharing her humour and enjoying her warmth. If ever a woman knew about the healing power of laughter it was Hermione.

At one moment Hermione had given me the chance of writing some material which she was planning to use in a two person revue with another English comic genius, Kenneth Williams. I worked hard to produce some sketches and songs which Hermione seemed to like. After some months of work the moment came to talk seriously with an impresario. The one chosen was the distinguished Peter Daubeney. Talks were under way when a phone call came from Sir Laurence Olivier in America. I happened to be with her at the time.

'Larry wants me to do a verse play touring in America, darling,' Hermione said calmly, before adding, 'I think Totie had better do it, we can always do the revue later.'

With that she gathered up her mink coat, her tooth brush and passport and with very little else in a tiny suitcase she flew off to what was to be a whole new phase of her career in America.

The verse play folded after a few weeks, but Hermione was spotted by a shrewd management scout and took over the Avis Bunnage role in *A Taste of Honey* which ran with enormous success on Broadway for another two years. Hermione, on a new wave of success, signed up with Walt Disney and was soon playing the cook in the famous film *Mary Poppins* with Julie Andrews. This made Totie an international name overnight. She then became a household name in America playing the maid, Maud, in a popular weekly TV series of the same name.

Hermione bought herself a beautiful home with a swimming pool in Beverly Hills as a setting for her new life. One day she found what she referred to as 'some funny people' in her garage. With her enormous intuition she rang the police and had them immediately moved on. The group of hippies then invaded the grounds of a nearby villa. Their leader turned out to be Charles Manson and the hideous Sharon Tate murder took place the following day.

Hermione, as everyone, was horrified by these events, and was soon to sell up and come back for a spell to Britain before finally acquiring another home near Hollywood. Meanwhile she was seriously thinking of settling back in Britain. So, having heard from me about my wooden house, she arrived that summer's day with the champagne as a house-warming present.

'Totie loves it here,' she said in her inimitable way as we sat in the wild garden. 'Are you sure Allon has really bought this lovely place? He's not telling fibs to keep Totie away?' She gave her gurgling laugh as I assured her I'd really bought it.

'Pity,' she added, looking round at my begonias radiating their brilliant hues of red and orange. Then she made me an offer to buy my house, as she fished in her hand-bag and produced her cheque book. I would have made a handsome profit. But I thought of the Messenger and the new purpose in my life. Hermione, as so many people, knew me as a writer and composer. I could not explain at that moment about the integral changes which were happening within me.

It was true that my theatre career still had things to offer. Soon after I was to have another production of my Oscar Wilde musical which was met with a good press, enthusiastic audiences and a desire to write another. Before I tackled the huge task of taming the wilderness about the house I made a long visit to France and came back with a new score and a new book, this time on an original theme of my own. Selling it was another matter. After preliminary attempts, I shelved it for the time being. As I worked at starting to clear the land about me, I meditated on the words of the Messenger. How could I forget them?

As if to occupy me whilst I was waiting for the Messenger's words to become reality, a whole new experience was dropped into my lap. Showing a neighbour over my house, he spotted some recently produced paintings which I had just framed. As he was at that time running the Sussex Gallery in Brighton, to my delight he offered me a one-man show. Having inherited the desire to paint from Grandfather Sewell, who was much admired for his skill as a painter in oils, I had already produced quite a lot of pictures in my more modern approach, using ink and colour on paper. My style is called figurative by the French. Having had no formal training I had picked up tips on technique from many sources. The art training at Rugby helped me a lot, in Cornwall I had worked a little alongside an artist, and, trained by my father to look at paintings since my early youth, I had absorbed a great deal. But it was the French who had really encouraged me to paint. Often in Paris, having spent the morning producing words, as a contrast I would spend the afternoons out in some corner with my sketch pad capturing a view which had inspired me. The French like creative people and I would sometimes sell a drawing from my pad as I worked. The thrill of a sale was enormous. I would order a special meal of coq au vin at my favourite *Restaurant Des Beaux Arts*, so near to where I lived in the rue de Seine.

In the South of France I had met Stephane Grappelli, and in Paris he demonstrated his genius in the healing power of music as well as showing me Montmartre. When we were not in the Club St Germain with his music flowing, we were visiting the country-like lanes of Montmartre exploring the ancient studios of the impressionists and the cubist painters. Braque, Manet, Monet, Van Gogh – their spirits seemed to breathe down my neck as I walked the old cobblestones, and stood by the fountain where they washed their brushes after a day's toil. I entered into the soul of *fin-de-siècle* Paris and was enriched.

I had helped a painter recover from a nervous breakdown by encouraging him to link with the life force and paint. His father knew and had shared mistresses and models with Lautrec. He taught me a technique of using ink line drawings and solid aquarelle which inspired me to further express myself on paper. To write is to observe, to paint is to observe. The psychic forces used by the creative side of man marry easily with the healing energies. All this I learned from the French.

For exercise after a midday meal I would walk. One of my favourite routes was and still is across the Pont des Arts, through the central court of the Louvre and along the rue de Rivoli to turn in towards the Palais Royale. There I walk under the famous arcades to stop in the gardens at the centre and gaze up at the window of the apartment where the great Colette lived, bed-ridden in her final years but still producing that personal style of prose hand-written on her blue paper. Often I saw the face of her spirit smiling down at me, those huge cat-like eyes framed by the wild hair.

Sometimes when funds and spirits were especially low, she seemed to call down to me, '*Courage, jeune homme,* have courage, young man, *un jour tu vas réussir,* one day you will make it.'

How I cherished those brief communications. I sent back my thanks to whatever world she might be in, still surrounded, I am certain, by her beloved dogs, cats and her collection of paper-weights in some flowered and shaded garden, still producing stories to enlighten and entertain her fellow souls.

It was therefore natural I would want to capture some of this rapport I had enjoyed with Colette and her work. I had once met her daughter, Colette de Juvenal, at a beach barbeque in St Tropez. Knowing she had lived for many summers there, I went searching for her villa which lies on the road towards Les Cannobières, a quiet beach curving round the bay beyond the town. Stopping my car outside the gates of *Les Treilles Muscat* I sat on its open hood and started to work on my picture. In my imagination I opened one of the metal gates as I gazed down the narrow path lined with foliage and dressed with the wire of the curved vine trellis partly revealing the charming pink-walled villa beyond. Within a short time the guardians of the villa appeared and in fact opened the gate for me to assist my work. Befriending me, and admiring my finished painting a few hours later, they invited me to the small guardians' lodge where, in perfect simplicity, I was invited to share their delicious dinner. The daughter of the family, a great beauty still in her teens, was studying astrology. Warming to her presence, I drew her, representing the young Colette in a dream-like composition to add to my exhibition. They made me a beautiful shepherd's waist-coat of wild wool, a garment I still have and cherish. So that summer I worked hard on my pictures.

One night I awoke in my flat in St Tropez to hear a gentle voice saying, 'Get up, look in the mirror, and draw what you see.'

Although it was two in the morning, I obeyed. I saw my face, solemn and pale with lack of sleep, yet coloured by the sun, gazing back at me. As I stared I saw another face behind mine, similar yet different. Taking my pen and crayons I tried to capture the second face. As I drew the chain and the cross I wore at that time about my neck, I knew the picture was to be called 'The Cross'. The next day as I went to the beach of Pamplonne to swim, I saw a group of hippies dressed in long robes standing near. Drawing the tallest, I sketched also some children kneeling staring at the tallest figure. That evening I drew in the curved river which I had approached in my fevered state those years ago in the sanatorium when, seeing the robed figure on the other side and my boat awaiting me, a hand on my shoulder had prefaced that strong voice which had forbidden me to cross. Thus I composed the full picture of the face behind mine staring out from the river and the boat in much smaller scale behind. The robed figure became Jesus teaching beside the Jordan to the enthralled children and adults gathered in awe silently about him. One man has a monkey on his shoulder.

When I had finished the picture my inner voice spoke again. 'You will exhibit this picture with the rest, but you must never sell it. It is an icon representing this stage of your spiritual progress, the stages you still have to work for, and the journey one day ahead of you.'

When I looked at the picture I rejoiced that my world felt at one. My creative work, my psychic sense, and my healing powers were joined in one expression. I was firing on all cylinders. I felt tremendously alive.

After gathering thirty-three pictures together in my wooden house, we realized that the gallery had been painted a colour which did not set them off well. So, having painted the pictures, I now had to set to with the others to paint the gallery. When Dame Flora Robson was handed her bouquet in thanks for opening the exhibition the paint on the walls was just dry.

I gave her one picture to be auctioned to help swell the fuel fund for the aged as Christmas was approaching. Although Lord Robin Maugham, the nephew of Somerset Maugham, bid high, it was finally the one-time famous newscaster, Leslie Mitchell, who bought it. As he was staying with friends who had asked me to treat him for a health problem, I told him to hang the picture, that of the famous Dr Brighton pub, within sight of his bed as a healing link should he ever be in need. He chuckled at the implied simile.

I had met Dame Flora several times at her home in Brighton and elsewhere and hearing that superb voice once again reminded me of her film performance as Elizabeth I of England, a role which has made its mark for all time.

I sold quite a few pictures, and many more afterwards as a result of the publicity. The whole preparation and event was important for me as a boost to my morale during the changing tides of my energy streams. Healing, writing, music, painting. I was grateful for the variety of my activities, but aware that I must not get lost. Praying for direction, the answer came clear and strong. 'Follow your healing star, and the rest will eventually fall into place.' As a tribute to my inner voice, I had not, in spite of a generous offer, sold the picture 'The Cross'. But I was soon to paint a new picture which was to act as a further link with the world of the spirit.

Whilst in Britain I had, whenever possible, remained faithful to my developing circle. After the advent of Nellie Quinlivan's healing, and the move to my wooden house as orchestrated by the Messenger, I knew my time to withdraw to my own setting for healing was approaching. I had served a long apprenticeship, as it were. I knew I was being prepared to go it alone. It was the arrival on my painting board of a new picture which was to confirm this.

In between my other activities, in preparation for receiving the sick and the troubled at 'Fairways', having made ready the house, I now had to finish taming the garden. The work was long and arduous. I rejoiced in the beautiful setting of my house in the valley. I planted over twenty cypress trees as wind-breaks, going out after storms to wash the salt off their tender stems as I encouraged them to grow tall and strong. A passing parks and gardens official shook his head when I idly discussed my plan for the garden.

'You won't get them to take well on this chalk.' He again shook his head.

But he had not reckoned on the healing hands and the prayer

power of the gardener. Soon my trees grew tall and strong, every single one of them. In the shelter of their evergreen barrier I dug and planted my vegetable patch. It was joyful, nourishing and economical to harvest my own potatoes, onions, broccoli, garlic, parsley and beans, to say nothing of gooseberries, the blackberries already in profusion and, later, apples, cucumbers and lettuce. I even made an arrangement with a local green-grocers to exchange any glut for anything else I might need. I supplied some of my friends with vegetables as well.

Meanwhile having to clear the ground of underground elder, stinging nettles and wild mint, I left great patches of wild grasses and purple flowers for the butterflies. Soon my garden was a paradise for wild flowers, birds and many glorious species of butterflies. I watched carefully for the flowers previously planted and cared for by Joyce Hassall, the wife of the previous occupier and mother to Paul, who had helped me find the owner that day, and his brothers and sisters. Little Simon often came panting up the hill with some delicious cake or sweet to add a homely touch to my table.

That next summer before leaving for France I painted some large panels to decorate my flat in St Tropez. I had already painted some irises which Hermione Baddeley bought and some roses, geraniums and lilies, and was preparing my painting board for a fuchsia I had encouraged to grow by the back verandah. I had set up the board, preparing it with its white foundation and I went to the kitchen to make myself a coffee. Turning about, mug of coffee in hand, I got a surprise. Standing beside my easel, arms akimbo, stripped to the waist, his wide shoulders in repose and wearing a single red feather as a symbol of the sacred flame standing upright at the back of his head, was the form of my friend 'Brave Spirit'. So many times had we met during meditation that I was used to seeing him on my inner third eye. This time he was showing himself for the first time objectively. His imposing spirit form exuded great energy. As he gazed straight into my eyes with an expression of calm and authority, I knew he wanted me to paint his picture.

Never having been trained as a portrait painter and having little experience of the media, I was just learning to use acrylic on board. I wondered what sort of a likeness I would be able to capture. But I knew I had to try. Putting the idea of painting the fuchsia aside, I asked for inspiration to tackle my new subject.

Mixing a pale brown wash on the plate which acted as a palette I set about roughly laying out the outline of the head and shoulders of the Indian appearing before me.

The next few hours, I can say the next few days, are fused in one memory. I must have eaten, and rested. All I can remember is working on that painting with all the concentration and energy I possessed. Away from my easel, unable to see my subject, I felt ill-at-ease. Then, as if knowing when he was needed to inspire me and act as a reference for his portrait, Brave Spirit showed himself. It was an extraordinary communion of souls as I worked to capture his likeness. Seeing the superb colours in the aura about his head, I tried to represent them in shafts of light. As I worked with a wide brush the strokes of paint became feather-like. I was thus taught, as research later proved, that the Indian tribesmen painted their feathers to represent their auras. The full radiant headdresses of the chieftain, of which Brave Spirit was one, demonstrated their spiritual evolvement by the magnificence of their headfeathers. I was thus inspired to portray what they instinctively demonstrated. In the communion of spirit I was illustrating my companion's thoughts. When the task was over, and I examined the result, I felt inadequate. I had painted more of an icon than a portrait, and yet some of the power of my visitor's personality stared back at me from the board. His brown eyes I had painted blue to try to capture the healing light which emanated from him. As I glanced to see if my visitor might be satisfied in any way by the result, he bowed deeply as if in gratitude for my efforts, and he was gone. As he faded I gave thanks for the time and energy he had spared. When I glanced back at the painting in a hand mirror to see it anew, I realized that the painting was a symbol of a deep experience. I knew I had drawn closer to one of my healing guides in spirit. I knew that I had advanced in attunement with the healing force emanating from the great White Cosmic Spirit. I remembered again the words of the messenger and I knew my painting activities had brought me full circle back to my life's purpose. I was further attuned to heal the sick and the troubled.

Knowing that I had already demonstrated the healing powers I had been given, I made a request in my meditative prayers that night. I wanted to be brought a case of healing of some physical symptom which I could see and touch and examine. I wanted to be made to believe what I already knew, that I was a healer. I needed to have it proven to me in all its simplicity. In answer to my request, it was soon to happen.

7.
MY FIRST STRANGER AS A PATIENT

I HAD been toiling away for hours on my now flourishing vegetable patch and decided to take a break at 'The Plough' in nearby Rottingdean. Pint in hand, I strolled outside to watch the ducks tipping up their tails searching the muddy water of the village pond for food.

'Wish we could do our shopping as simply,' said a tall, slim, young man who had come up beside me. His black hair was cut Beatle fashion. His handsome face looked troubled. He wore dark glasses.

'This light is disturbing me,' he said. 'Why don't we go back into the pub and chat?'

'Of course,' I said, hesitant to leave the beauty of the setting, but responding instinctively to some quality in the young man.

'By the way, I'm Clive Hill,' he added casually.

I introduced myself as we found a corner inside and asked, 'Better here?'

'Yes, a little. Sorry to bore you but I don't feel too well. I can't stand strong light.'

Glancing at the dark-beamed interior, I asked 'Since when?'

'Since a car accident.' He gave me some details of the accident and continued, 'The doctors don't seem to be able to do much for me. I get flashing lights across my vision, my stomach hurts, my shoulder is bad, I can't sleep. I'm a wreck.' Gulping from his beer mug, he smiled wanly.

'Sounds miserable,' I replied, wishing I could help the man.

'Actually,' he added, 'I'm looking for a healer. I'll try anything. You don't by any chance happen to know one, do you?'

I caught my breath as I studied his pale face. I somehow felt this chance meeting with a stranger was not an accident. I reacted to the challenge as calmly as I could.

'You're looking at one.'

Clive gave my muddy boots and blue jeans a quick survey, removed his dark glasses and stared at me for a moment. Without further pause he said, 'Well then, let's go.'

Twenty minutes later Clive was sitting in the simple wooden chair I had placed in the centre room of my house waiting for my first patient. I asked him to relax as he talked more about the accident, telling how as a keen driver and a small-part actor, his whole life had been upset by the ill health which had recently dogged him. In a moment of prayer I asked silently that I might be of service to him. I rested my hands on his shoulders and felt the healing energy flow through them.

'That feels good,' Clive responded immediately. He went into the relaxed silence that patients often enjoy while receiving healing, as I charged up his energy centres and worked my hands slowly about his head and spine. After treating his shoulder, I closed the healing as I often do by making the sign of the cross over Clive's head. After a short rest he thanked me and was gone. Two days later he rang to tell me he felt like a different man.

It was the sequel to this which brought about the moment I had been waiting for. Some time later Clive rang me to say he had quite another problem. I gave him an appointment for that afternoon to find that now he had a lump over his windpipe. I examined him carefully. Just below and to one side of his vocal chords, the lump – the size of a small bird's egg – felt like a hard, round, smooth ball of a swelling, slightly mobile to the touch. It sat in a pouch of skin near to his Adam's apple.

'How long has this been here?' I asked.

'Some weeks now it's been growing,' he said. 'The doctor I've seen wants an operation. I have a bed booked in the Royal Sussex Hospital. But suddenly I remembered you and how much you had helped me.'

He looked up in hope. As I gently examined him I realized that this was the moment I had been primed for.

Here was a physical symptom clearly visible and tangible, already examined by a doctor, about to be operated on. Instead Clive had come to me first for the laying on of hands. I knew in my heart that this was the moment of proof if the powers around me were to use me as an instrument of healing. This was no 'could be,' or 'might be,' or psychosomatic headache or anything ephemeral. Here was a specific physical symptom challenging me as a healer to remove it by the healing power.

I stood behind Clive sitting in the wooden chair and breathed in the Holy Spirit. I was aware of my consciousness rising up to link with the Cosmic Force available for me. When I was ready I placed the tips of my fingers gently about the lump on Clive's throat. I asked silently that I might be allowed the proof I needed to give me the total confidence I sought in my work. I do not know how long I stayed in this state of apartness.

When it was over, I became aware once more of myself and of Clive resting quietly in the healing chair. We shared a pot of tea made with tea and mint from the garden and chatted. Then he left me. The next day I busied myself with the daily chores of life as I waited anxiously to hear from him.

It was three days later that Clive phoned to tell me his dramatic news. He had gone back to his family home in Hove. Complaining suddenly of aching and sweating, he had been put to bed by his mother. The following two days he lay in bed still sweating and aching as if, he told me, he were suffering from influenza. But the next day he got up to find his body strong. Examining his throat in the shaving mirror he found that the lump had shrivelled from the size of a bird's egg to that of a very small pea.

When the time came for him to enter the Royal Sussex Hospital for his operation, his doctor naturally gave him another examination. He found the lump had all but disappeared. He searched for a scar and, mystified on finding none, asked how Clive had got rid of the problem. Clive said he had told the doctor the truth, that he had been to a spiritual healer. The doctor smiled and shook his head in wonder. He washed his hands and announced that the operation was no longer necessary.

At my bidding Clive called on me so that I could see the truth for myself. Clive's mother had witnessed the change, as had his grandmother, and the doctor. Now it was my turn. As I looked at and touched Clive's throat, I saw that the lump which had been there a few days before was now virtually gone, shrunk to almost nothing.

As I examined it, I gave thanks for Clive's sake – and for my own. The proof of my healing talent had been established to my satisfaction. I was a healer. God had once again manifested His healing power, this time through myself, with the aid, I believe, of my guardian angels. I was ready to go public. There would be no more hesitancy or hiding the truth. I had taken great pains to keep quiet the story of Nellie Quinlivan, but I was ready to tell the Clive Hill story to anyone who might be interested. I knew that my long years of apprenticeship were over. My visions, my guides were all being proved correct. I had obeyed the Messenger and his message was already unfolding. I was chosen as the instrument for many more wonderful things to follow. As a healer I had only just begun.

Through word of mouth, people got to hear of my healing powers. There was no wild rush at first, but a steady trickle of people seeking my help. After being vouched for by Stewart Lawson, a well-known healer and medium, and after having four of my healing cases put on paper, witnessed and examined, I was accepted as a fully-practising member of the National Federation of Spiritual Healers, one of the largest and most respected body of healers in Great Britain.

As a result of these events, I was interviewed on BBC Radio Brighton. This created such interest that after three days the radio authorities had to ask the public to free the telephone lines for their out-going calls.

One man who wrote asking to meet me was a Tony Scantlebury who lived in Hollingbury, a district of Brighton not far from my home. I will always remember the quiet courage and the dignity of this man, about forty, of medium and compact build, as he walked into my sanctuary and took the chair offered him.

'What can I do for you?' I asked him, noting the seriousness of his look.

'I've been given less than a year to live. I am a married man. For the sake of my wife and children I must do all I can to help myself.' I noticed the slight local accent to his voice and his strong working-man's hands.

'I understand.' As I spoke I felt desperately sorry for this human being, so composed at such a time. I knew it was not pity he needed, but action. 'Tell me all you can.'

I sat quietly as Tony told me his story in simple words. He had been admitted to hospital suffering from stomach pains. After examinations, tests and X-rays, an exploratory operation was decided upon. But the day before planned surgery, 'The doctor decided to leave well alone. I was developing a swelling which was eventually the size of another stomach. I lost two stone in weight. Then they arranged for a body scan.'

I knew that Brighton had recently acquired one of the latest and finest body scanners in the country.

'After the scan they told me,' Tony went on, 'that there is an in-operable growth over my pancreas. They sent me home. They told me there is no more they can do.' Tony paused as he looked calmly at me. 'All that a few days ago. Then I heard your broadcast.'

As I listened I asked my spirit guides and helpers to use me as the healing instrument. I thought of his young wife and children waiting for him at his home. An enormous desire to help flooded my being.

'Well, I can offer you what you seek, the laying on of hands.' I said, quietly. 'The rest is out of my hands.' I realized then the implication of these words, to be given to me later for my book's title.

'So let's get to work.'

As I asked Tony to lift up his pullover I saw more clearly the huge swelling in the stomach area preventing him from closing the waist-band of his trousers, secured by a wide belt. Placing one hand on the swelling and the other in the middle of his back I set about healing. I remember being inspired to circle his waist with my hands, moving slowly so that every part of the growth would be submitted to the energy I sensed flowing from me. Tony was later to describe the event thus: 'I was surprised to feel heat like that of an electric blanket coming from Allon's hands, but only in the region of the affected area.'

So it was that the first of many healing sessions took place. Tony's name went onto my absent healing list to receive healing prayers night and morning as had been my daily custom these many moons. The weeks went by.

We did not say much about it at first, not wishing to exaggerate or pin our hopes falsely. But after a few weeks we both knew the swelling was subsiding, because the strain on the belt at Tony's waist was noticeably less. Within a month or so he was able to button up his trouser-waist, and the muscle tone was returning to his abdominals. Tony spoke later about his new condition. 'I put on weight and began to sleep better *and* on the side which was formerly painful.'

After a further medical examination Tony reported, 'The doctor prodded me, seemingly looking for the growth he did not appear to find. A second body scan was requested.'

Meanwhile Tony saw again the doctor on duty at his place of work who had since read the specialist's report. After close questioning the work doctor confirmed, 'They had suspected a tumour across the pancreas in the liver area.'

Surprised at Tony's improvement, the doctors then told him his condition might have been inflammatory, and, before issuing a final report, they ordered a third body scan. The result of this third scan, to quote again Tony's words, was, 'The doctor confirmed to me the first scan had shown a solid mass which was not now apparent. On questioning him he told me the original solid mass was thought to be cancer.' After Tony had come to me for healing, the greatly swollen pancreas was now 'about one tenth of the size it was when it contained the solid growth' according to the doctors.

Speaking later to the *Psychic News* reporter who wrote up the story, Tony said, 'Despite their skill and kindness the doctors had to tell me my case was hopeless. Owing to spiritual healing's wonderful power I feel my life has been saved. The peace and calm which first came to me on visiting Allon has never left me.'

Ever since those events in 1979 I receive a simply worded Christmas card from Tony Scantlebury reminding me of his wonderful healing which we were both privileged to share. And every year he pays me a welcome visit.

I never guessed that my healing hands would bring me next into touching fingers with the Beatles legend. It happened without my realizing it.

As I wrote the name Lennon on my telephone pad I did not heed the implication. I did register from the sadness and hesitancy of the woman's voice that here was another human being in distress seeking my help. One look at the attractive blonde who walked into my sanctuary at the appointed time confirmed my impression – the young woman was in deep depression. As I offered her the chair beside mine in my snuggery I could feel the tension and despair emanating from Pauline Lennon to darken her aura.

'My husband died some months ago,' she said quietly with

bowed head. 'It's left me feeling terrible,' she added, with an alarming emphasis on the final word.

'Only those who have suffered grief through loss of a loved one can understand.'

'I thought of the pain I had lived through after the death of my mother. Then I remembered the comfort I had experienced when she appeared to me afterwards, serene, confident. I prayed that a similar comunication might manifest to help my visitor. Then it happened.

I saw, on the small screen of my third eye, a man's face – long, slim features, short grey hair.

'Tell Pauline not to grieve my death. Tell her she must start to live again. Our love is still there.'

I gave Pauline the impressions I was receiving. She listened attentively but in silence. As I watched my small screen I saw the man was showing me an X-ray of his body. Telling me he had died of cancer, he showed me how it had spread and how the surgeon had only discovered the extent of the disease too late to save him – at any rate, an impossible task.

'No-one knows this except me and him and the doctor – I told no-one.' Pauline spoke through her tears.

'I am telling you this to prove life goes on after death. Make her realize. Make her want to go on living,' the man was insisting. I relayed his thoughts to Pauline.

'This man had to die, he is explaining to me, it was his time. But not yours.' Pauline sat silent.

Then the man said to me, 'Tell David I don't want him to smoke. David, my son, ask her to tell him.'

At the name of David, Pauline sat up in her chair as if something had lifted her physically.

'Then it must be Freddie – the description of his growth, the way you described his features – now the name of David, our son. I left him in his pram in your garden. It must indeed be my husband.' Pauline almost cried out with joy as the grief left her. I watched her literally stepping back into life.

A few days later Pauline wrote to me.

As he was older than I, my husband (Freddie) was all things to me, and so when the inevitable occurred it meant the learning of a very hard lesson for me. This was when your help came in, giving me the strength to carry on ... What you did for me was to direct a crisis experience into a positive enlightening thing which has resulted in spiritual development. Without your guidance it might have had a negative, embittering effect. My thoughts are with you and all those you are helping. When I feel agitated or confused I look at the peace and steadiness which emanates from you.

Touched by this, it was later I discovered that the man Frederick who had communicated with me from the next world was indeed Beatle John Lennon's father, making Pauline his step-mother.

Whilst meeting Pauline a year or so later I 'saw' another man with white football socks and brown, curly hair whom I felt might be featuring in her life. They have since married. We have all become friends and on dining with them recently Pauline, 'Socks' and I all raised our glasses to Yoko, who had sent the wine in a Christmas hamper.

As a writer I naturally took notes on the events which were happening to me. Then, one Sunday morning on waking, I recalled an instruction which I had a moment before in sleep received from one of my guides.

'To share your story with many you will produce a book on your healing powers. It will help many people. You will call it *Out of My Hands* and you will start today.'

I obeyed. Within a few months my story was on paper, an early manuscript version of this book. Owing to publicity in the London-based weekly *Psychic News*, followed by the seeming coincidence of meeting the right people at the right time, a digest of my book was published in *Woman's Own*, a magazine of enormous circulation in the United Kingdom and the Commonwealth. It was serialized in two parts; a new exciting experience to see myself and my healing hands illustrated right across a centre-page double-spread.

'Here's your fan-mail, Mr Bacon,' the postman said, dropping a huge bundle of letters at my feet as I was trimming a tree in my garden. The letters came from all over Britain and Ireland, and from France, Poland, Germany, the US, Canada, South Africa, Australia – well over two thousand of them.

'You look as if you need some help,' said Dottie Bonnin, another patient with a health problem which improved after healing. As a trained secretary, her help was gratefully received, and has been ever since.

People came to me in cars and on foot. Some drove south from Yorkshire, hoping to see me without even an appointment. Some phoned incessantly or put messages through my front door. Some African women, superb in their flowing dashiki and huge turbans waited to touch me as I crossed my garden. The switchboard of Radio Brighton was busy again after another interview with me.

I had to accept that my fame was spreading. The Messenger had been right. I also realized I could only receive for healing relatively few of the numbers who sought me. I planned to reach many more with future writings and lecturing. And so it has evolved.

If the sick and the troubled were beating a path to my door as the Messenger had told me they would, I too responded to chances to go out to spread the word. I shared the platform for my first public healing demonstration in my home town, where I not only spoke but also put my hands to work. The event was a success and made a profit for the Federation (NFSH) but left many unanswered questions in my mind. Although I talked briefly with the sick who came up to the platform for healing, the conversation was purposely amplified by microphone to the hall and made the lack of intimacy a challenge. The big question for me was, what happened afterwards to the people who received benefit? There is no follow-up to public healing. One dear old lady waddled up on two sticks to my healing stool and, having received her treatment, walked easily off the platform with tears accompanied by applause. She even raced back for her forgotten sticks before disappearing from my sight. I often think of her and how she fared. I send her prayers even as I write.

My next important opportunity to do platform work was when I was invited to write and give a paper on behalf of the NFSH at the Holistic Healing Conference at Loughborough University. It was fascinating to be sharing the platform with several doctors and other therapists as well as the ever young Sir George Trevelyan who has given such energy to help launch the Wrekin Trust, a wide adult education organization geared to teaching the eternal knowledge to the New Age. As I stood there, confident and fit, having conquered the inevitable nerves which presage one's first important public lecture, a part of me rejoiced. I have since lectured and healed in public so many times, but nothing can erase the memory of that first talk surrounded by doctors. As my opening words launched out into the hall I was wonderfully aware of their significance. For, but for destiny, I would, as I told my audience, have hopefully become a doctor myself had I not those years before as a medical student succumbed to the illness which dramatically changed my path by inspiring my powers to conquer it. And now I was telling doctors my idea of how to use my self-tested healing on others. Perhaps for the first time, the significance of my opening sentence lit up my soul, 'I became a healer through falling ill – if that sounds contradictory, it was meant to . . .'

Truly my cup was full and brimming over.

8.
HOW DOES SPIRITUAL HEALING WORK?

It was my first meeting with Marlene Dietrich which inspired me to learn a great deal about how spiritual healing works. That statement might surprise a lot of people. It was meant to. I will elaborate.

It was during the sixties, when I was deeply involved in developing my healing powers, that I became aware that there are living amongst us people who have learned to transmit and share their etheric energies which are of a higher ratio than the average. I had heard about Dietrich's recent emergence with a one-woman show whilst in Paris writing a musical. The seats at the Châtelet theatre were too highly priced for my resources so I had to wait until she played the Theatre Royal, Brighton, before I was able to see her. Because her birthday, December 27th, is three days after mine on Christmas Eve, I had always felt an affinity with this fellow Capricorn. I understand the basically lone trail it is our destiny to plod, and the courage within which is available to us to fulfil whatever our destiny can offer. To register my admiration for this particular Capricorn, I sent Dietrich a fairly humble bunch of flowers and a note saying I was looking forward to seeing her show. Two days later, to my astonishment, she rang me up and invited me to meet her after her Saturday night performance, which I was to attend.

Knowing her age and the extraordinary career she had carved out for herself since her emergence as a star in *Blue Angel* as a rather plump but beautiful young woman who then conquered Hollywood and the world's cinema screens, I was not expecting the vision she presented to us. Wearing a long closely-fitting dress shimmering like gossamer and trailing her swans-down fur cape of huge proportions, she unveiled for us a vision of youth and beauty which was compelling.

I knew some of the tricks this clever woman used to create her superb image on stage. I knew the dresser at the Châtelet in Paris had fainted on finding what she thought was Dietrich hanging up in the wardrobe, when it in fact was her working gown filled out here and there to fool the eye of the beholder. So what? What I did not expect on seeing La Dietrich on stage was the light I saw about her. Over and above the stage lighting, the pink spot and all the effects a modern switchboard can produce, I saw something else. My third eye registered an etheric light about her head and shoulders which carried an angelic glow. I saw the white light of high intensity which Dietrich could produce on stage to dazzle, bewitch and charm her audience. This was not just an ageing beauty looking good by using every resource that time, attention to detail and money could effect. This was a phenomenon of much more subtle a kind. I was watching that night the radiance of spirit which this woman had been given to fulfil her extraordinary role. Dietrich was giving out much more than her artistry of voice, movement and interpretation of song. She was giving, in her individual manner, spiritual energy. She was handing out courage and hope to every ageing woman in the audience, an example to the young ones, and a spiritual lift to every man. That is apart from her timeless sex appeal.

I learned that night that great stars have great luminosity. I learned that great entertainers diffuse great incandescence. They have blazing auras which give out and receive great energy, and in the case of Dietrich, a part of this energy was giving healing. Whether she knew it or not, her audience was not just being entertained, it was having its individual auras charged up. And this charging up of our individual auras, by one method or another, is the basis of spiritual healing.

When, back-stage a few minutes after the fall of the curtain, I met Dietrich, my comprehension of her magic spell was confirmed. As she approached me, glass of whisky in hand, cigarette also, to shake my hand with her free one, I met quite a different woman to the vision she had just created. Dressed now in a dark, neatly-tailored Chanel-like suit and white stockings and wearing little make-up but lipstick and eye lashes, she was the efficient cosmopolitan woman doing her public relations job.

'I am glad you love Paris,' she said directly to me in that fascinating deep voice. 'I live in the Avenue Montaigne, and I love it too.' Her presence seemed then to flash various images to grip my attention. She radiated the businesswoman, then the sex symbol, the artist and the survivor. All to capture my interest.

'Burt Bacharach is a genius,' she added, whilst talking to me about music. I knew his wonderful new arrangements had re-launched her recording career .

I knew too I had been singled out to please, to mentally seduce and to meet because I was at the right place at the right time making the right noises. She had sensed my desire to meet her and acted upon it. She knew too that everywhere she went, people must be chosen to meet, to conquer. I had been chosen. She knew I would tell people about the meeting. Such is the desire of a great star to work at their image. I consider I have done her's proud. And she did me a great service. She demonstrated to me in clear terms the power of the human aura. Thank you, Dietrich. I send you at this moment of time my healing prayers, to help you survive the problems of retirement and change which I hear you are having to face.

Man has always known about the human aura. The ancients always pictured the saints as having a halo about their heads. Fra Angelico, a primitive Italian painter, pictured holy people as having golden circles of light about their heads to represent their shining spiritually-advanced auras. Every one of us has an aura which by its qualities of colour, brightness and density represents our true state of being. If we are tired, for example, our auras are less brilliant. Positive, successful people have bright auras which light up the space about them. Their etheric bodies are charged.

Modern scientists sometimes refer to the etheric body as the bio-physical body. We all carry this etheric energy field which emanates within and about us, extending to a few inches or more about us. When we die we take a part of this energy field with us, the part which houses our soul – our spiritual counterpart. The physical body is born attached to the umbilical cord linking it with its mother before it is severed. On death our etheric body, linked in part with our field force, is free to float away, attached by a silver cord which is finally severed. Thus the physical body, bereft of its life force, dies. Being now useless, it is disposed of, whilst the spiritual body, now freed, moves onto a new existence on a higher plane of vibration.

When our physical bodies are in harmony with our balanced

spiritual bodies, we are well. A shock to the etheric body can manifest in turn as disease to the physical body. Any infection to the physical body in turn affects the harmony of the etheric body. Likewise any illness or injury or shock to the physical body has to be registered by the etheric body, for it is one whole structure.

Man is not just the visible, tangible, physical body with a skeletal structure, a blood system and a muscle system controlled by the linking nerves energized by the brain. Man is also mind, emotion, and in his spiritual centre, soul. Any one of these physical or etheric or mental departments is affected by any other.

The eastern religions teach us about the Yin and the Yang, the complementary life forces which run throughout the physical body of man and can be likened to an invisible electric wiring system carrying the life energies. Illness and injury block the flow of these energies. Spiritual healing can give a corrective, de-blocking effect, allowing the natural flow to be re-instated. Spiritual or psychic healing can inspire the de-harmonized etheric body of man to re-instate its harmonic pattern, which in turn triggers off changes in the closely-linked physical body.

Other techniques such as acupuncture (the use of needles or pressure at appointed places to encourage the energy flow), or reflexology (foot massage used for the same purpose) and many more can be used to achieve the reinstatement of harmony in the body of man. But the purpose of this book is to discuss spiritual healing.

It could be said that the use of drugs as practised in allopathic medicine encourages the body to place itself back in the harmony of health using chemcial means. Whichever way we look at the process of healing, we reach a moment of mystery. The moment when the body itself regains its harmony as the essential life force flows freely once more and the miracle of the human being reverts to its own fundamental plan. If we have a scientific attitude we can explain this in terms of chemicals, amino-acids and so forth. If we have a religious attitude we might refer to the idea that the body and the spirit of man is reflecting his Divine Blueprint. God made us perfect; we are reclaiming this right by a spiritual exercise. But this spiritual exercise involves the use of energy, which in turn affects the harmonizing of the etheric body linked with the physical. Once again we arrive at trying to understand the mystery of prayer.

Healing prayer can be likened to the intake of Divine Energy allowing us to right our etheric body and so the physical body.

'Mind over matter', as it is seen by possibly non-religious believers, can also explain the re-harmonizing of the bio-plasmic body in turn linked with the physical.

As a spiritual healer I see the process of healing as the technique of allowing myself as a medium to tune into the Cosmic Energy available to us all, and thus to channel this corrective energy towards the patient. When my patients feel the warmth flowing from my hands into the affected part of them, they are sensing the energy boost.

At times one of my hands registers cold on the patient and the other hot. This leads me to believe in simplistic terms that the healing energy is an electric or electro-magnetic energy which in some way corrects the disharmony in the etheric and so the physical body, in part or in whole, of the patient.

When I am healing, more often than not, I see a flow of fine smoke-like substance rising up from my fingers. I believe I see this with my third eye, but it is difficult for me to judge as in this case the vision from my physical eye corresponds. When I am giving healing to the head chakra of the patient, I often see this 'smoke' flowing from my hands to mingle with another similar column of like substance issuing from the patient's head. I call this 'my spiritual bonfire', as if I am helping to draw out some waste matter from the patient to be replaced by new energy. Depression cases seem to give out a lot of this waste as they have their brain rhythms changed to positive from the negative state in which I found them. But remember, every time I make an observation of like nature, I am aware that as a healer I am also a student. The wondrous knowledge of the functioning of spiritual and physical man is awe-inspiring. On planet Earth we are merely scratching the surface of further knowledge waiting for us elsewhere. But I am certain that if we ask in sincerity we will be allowed to broaden our experience, our expertise, and our knowledge. The action of healing brings the understanding. So we hopefully progress. Ask and we shall receive.

Let us look more closely at the phenomena we have mentioned – the etheric body, and its properties, followed by a study of brain rhythms.

The Etheric or Bio-physical Body

What scientific evidence have we available to back up the knowledge of the presence of man's etheric body? As far back as the turn of the century, Dr Kilner, working at St Thomas' Hospital, London, as a specialist in the use of electro-therapy, produced evidence concerning the human aura which created great interest, to say the least. He discovered that by looking at the physical body of a patient through a lens treated with a coal-tar dye called dicyanin he could distinguish another body stretching from six to eight inches beyond the solid form. Because his special lens could perceive into the ultra-violet range of light he described this hitherto invisible extra body as a cloud about the patient. Dr Kilner observed that this cloud, now referred to as the bio-plasmic body, varied from patient to patient. After examining many hundreds of patients in this way, he was able to note changes in this etheric body brought about by disease in the physical body of the same patient. He went further, and learned to diagnose, for example, cancer of the cervix in women, which in certain cases he could foretell. It seems astonishing to me that this doctor's findings, so advanced in time, should not have maintained the interest they created; particularly as he presented his discoveries in a scientific manner unhampered by theological arguments or censorship which an added belief in Spiritualism, for example, might have brought. Dr Kilner produced impressive evidence that the etheric body of man was a fact. His additional discovery, that disease present or being cured in the physical body of the patient was also reflected in the etheric body, is to me, as a healer, of enormous significance.

It was not until 1939 that a further breakthrough in the examination of the human and other auras happened. The place was Krasnodar near the Black Sea in Southern Russia. The man an electrical engineer, Semyon Kirlian. On his way to pick up some equipment for repair, he happened upon a demonstration of the use of a high-frequency instrument used for electro-therapy. On seeing a flash of light between the electrodes and the patient's body, Kirlian became fascinated in the idea of photographing this manifestation. As so often with pioneers, he risked personal injury in the manner in which he proceeded with his experiments. Dangerously using metal electrodes in place of the previously observed glass ones, Kirlian avoided the error of having his photographic plate spoiled by the light which the glass would have allowed to pass through it. So the spark caused by the electrodes lit up his hand as well as causing an impression of it straight onto a photographic plate without the need of a camera. In this way Kirlian was thrilled to find he had recorded not only a photograph of his hand but also of the energy field which manifested about it. Working closely with his wife, Valentina, a teacher and journalist, Semyon quickly evolved a more sophisticated technique using his newly-built high-frequency spark generator.

The first photograph which Kirlian took with his new apparatus was that of a leaf. A blue-green and yellow ochre light was seen to be issuing from certain parts of the leaf. A human finger seemed to have a light glowing from within. Not wishing to be limited to photographing these phenomena, the Kirlians developed an optical instrument for examining these newly-found bodies of light in motion. With their newly named optoscope, the full wonder of their discoveries opened up to them. A whole new world of beauty and wonder was theirs to examine. The human hand and its accompanying etheric double took on the appearance of a multi-coloured ever-moving mass of various lights and flashes all united in one amazing ensemble. The age-old mystery of the human aura was examined and seen to be a moving field of energy, colour and light, ever-changing in its intensity and appearance. So a leaf was seen to give off its own moving mass of light whilst living, less whilst dying, and none when dead.

The Kirlians were in this way to prove what the ancients had always known, that everything living has its aura. The ancients had been correct to pray to the living gods of the trees, the waters, and all living matter about them. As modern scientists have long realized, the heart of the atom beats in unity whether it is the atom in the body of man or in nature or in the ether. All living bodies have an etheric counterpart. Such is the mystery of life as seen by the scientists. And the Kirlians played a vital part in the unfolding of this knowledge to modern man. Thus the scientists had proven what folklore had always known, that man carried within, without, and about him his own etheric or bio-physical double. Spiritual man became a fact. Man was known to be more than flesh and blood; he carried also his own built-in ghost.

To summarize, it seems probable that the effect of healing energies on man's etheric double, linked as it is with his physical body, and linked as they both are with his mind and his soul identity, bring about the creative change we call spiritual (or psychic) healing.

When I was invited to give healing at Olympia, London, for the Festival of Mind and Body in 1978, I had the opportunity of having a Kirlian photograph made of my hands. Thus for the first time I saw a physical trace on paper of my healing energies, something I had only previously seen with my third eye. Thus science and the occult link up. When Brian Snellgrove, a specialist in the reading of hand auras who has learned to recognize traits of talent and life pattern as shown therein, examined my Kirlian photograph he commented, 'You are a man of many parts – but your healing is essential.' And so it is.

The Head Chakra and Brain Rhythms

We have already learned that the head chakra, one of the seven centres of energy in the etheric body of man, is, by its link with the brain, of vital significance. The brain houses the mind, and is therefore the control centre for conscious and unconscious decisions concerning the deportment and behaviour of man. The head chakra, linked as it is with the brain, services many other more widely significant purposes. Its use, both in reception as an aerial and in transmission as a receiver, has enormous known and unknown power and potential. The electro-magnetic vibrations generated in the brain not only play an important part in the etheric body of man, they also generate rhythms of energy which can affect other head chakras near or far. Herein lies the secret of the process known as the power of persuasion, brought about as it is by the power of personality. We have already discussed the power of the star personality on others. This power, to a greater or lesser degree, is present in people in countless walks of existence. The politician and the leaders of men can obviously be cited as generating above-average head energies. It may surprise you to learn that a developed psychic gives out up to fifty times more energy than the average person from the back of his brain. Scientists call this energy the psi factor. As developed psychics, spiritual or psychic healers have this boosted energy pattern. Destiny has supplied them with the necessary potential to exercise their healing powers. If certain psychics choose to use this power to move match-boxes under test conditions, to bend spoons or to move tables – whatever the fashion of the day – that is their choice. Spiritual healers are inspired by their innate compassion for the sick and the troubled to use their special energies to repair lives and comfort souls. Everybody to their particular activity of the moment. Let us study more about brain rhythms, their structure and performance.

Brain Rhythms

As far back as the thirties in apparatus called the electro-encephalogram – known for convenience as the EEG – was invented by medical scientists to examine human brain waves. The electrical waves manufactured by the brain are very slight and they have to be stepped up four million times to be detected on the EEG. This machine is able to react to these waves and translate its reception of them into the tracing of their density by a visible graph registered on a slowly revolving roll of paper on a horizontal drum. Thus an invisible force is made measurable by the human eye. Doctors found this machine of enormous value whilst examining, for example, cases of epilepsy, brain tumours, and brain damage following accidents.

Two or three decades passed before a scientist and doctor called Maxwell Cade, working with an electronics expert Geoffrey Blundell, married the EEG machine to a scanning screen. The result was that instead of brain rhythms being recorded as a frozen graph they could now be seen as a living pattern representing more closely what they in fact are. The two men called their new invention 'The Mind Mirror'. It was whilst giving healing at The Festival of Mind and Body in London that I was wired up to this new machine before a group of people. As a patient was brought to me, I raised my consciousness according to my usual technique before giving the laying on of hands. As the scanner of the machine examining me was alongside me, I was able for the first time with my human eyes to see the effect of the healing process on my own brain rhythms. What I learned from this experience was very valuable to me in moving further towards understanding the mystery of spiritual healing. Although I give here the report written on this examination by Maxwell Cade himself, my own realization of the event was crucial. I had studied healing, I had practised healing, now I was witnessing the creation of my healing brain waves. I lived through a moment of intellectual and spiritual expansion never to be forgotten. Seeing is believing, and I saw and believed.

The following document on my brain rhythms is of interest.

Allon Bacon

The measurements taken at the 1978 Festival of Mind and Body of Allon Bacon's brain rhythms during healing were found to be of the following unusual form:-

Left and Right hemispheres

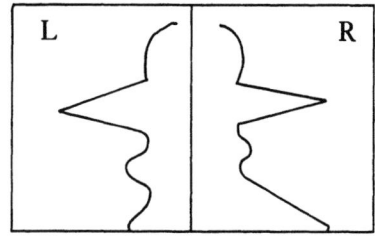

16 Hz   Beta

9 Hz   Alpha

3–2 Hz   Delta

This pattern shows the Fifth State (The Awakened Mind, or Nirbikalpa Samadhi) with the exception that it shows very strong right delta waves and very weak delta waves on the left. The meaning of this is that the left half of the brain (the normal intellectual functions) is not operating, whereas the right half of the brain (intuitive processes) is, and one can infer from this that you are making intuitive assessments concerning your patient.

This is the highest healing state which we have been able to measure, and what it means is that you are able to bring all your normal physical and mental powers effectively to bear in the 'meditative' state. You can, for example, move about and talk to your patients without any loss of healing power, whereas healers who are confined to lower states find it necessary to keep still and silent for their healing to be effective.

Report by C. Maxwell Cade

NOTES TO HELP THE READER UNDERSTAND THE BRAIN RHYTHM PATTERNS

Scientists studying brain rhythms have come up with their own specialized jargon on the subject, that is to say, they divide them into alpha, beta, theta and delta waves, according to their quality. They are also read off on the Hz scale, Hz meaning frequency in cycles per second.

Beta is the normal waking rhythm of the brain associated with active thinking, etc.

Alpha is the most prominent rhythm but can only be interpreted when one knows the others.

Theta appears as consciousness slips towards drowsiness.

Delta is primarily associated with deep sleep. Delta waves have also been reported at the onset of paranormal phenomena.

Once we have started to understand the form and the functions of the etheric body of man and of his brain rhythms, a whole new attitude to the mysteries of spiritual healing is opened up to us. Processes which were hitherto inexplicable become within the grasp of comprehension. We take a step nearer to understanding the functioning of miracles. They are the result of processes which were at one time beyond our analysing. That in no way takes away the wonder of them. Seen through the eyes of a man of faith a miracle is a happening brought about by his God. The same happening seen through the eyes of a scientist need not be any less wonderful. The laws and workings of science have their own superb revelations. Whether a scientist has faith in his God or not does not matter; the laws of science remain. Only their interpretation differs.

Carl Jung, whom I consider to be one of the greatest minds of this century, had the following words in Latin carved over the front door of his house: *Vocatus atque non, vocatus Deus aderit*, which being translated mean 'Whether you invite God into your house or not, no matter, He is already there.'

Prayer

Now that we have started to examine the theory that spiritual healing works through the impinging of energies given out by the healer on the etheric and so the physical body of the patient, let us take another look at the process we call prayer.

Prayer is the organized use of energy. This energy can be described as bio-physical, etheric, spiritual, or possibly electro-magnetic, depending on the discipline or attitude of the spokesman. Prayer, to many, is attunement to their God. To others it is the deliberate projection of thought waves for a specific purpose. To a healer this purpose is healing. How does it work?

Curiously enough a moment of insight flashed into my mind concerning prayer during a pause in a radio broadcast. I was being interviewed, not for the first time, on my local radio network, then called Radio Brighton, by its leading light, Bob Gummel. As the formula of the hour-long broadcast consisted of Bob interviewing me in between my choice of records, we had time to chat privately whilst the music was being played. I had the pleasure of demonstrating my wide taste in music by choosing examples of the classics, operatic arias, jazz and musical comedy as well as a private recording made in the theatre of a song from a show of mine. I was thus enjoying a moment of gratitude for having been inspired to write this particular song called *England in Summertime*, which had already delighted many thousands of people, when another mind-inspiring thought struck me. As the music played I sent out a healing prayer to all those listening who might benefit from it. In return, as if as a thank you from some angelic source, I received in a flash an understanding of the sending and receiving of prayer thoughts.

As in broadcasting our physical voice is translated into electronic vibrations sent invisibly and silently across the ether to be picked up by the radio receiver and thus translated back into audible sound for the ear of the listener, likewise the sending of prayer. It is the generating of a thought energy form sent invisibly and silently on an even higher vibration than radio waves to an even finer receiver, the head chakra of the receiver who may or may not be conscious of its reception. Nevertheless the reception of this thought energy called prayer can cause a reaction in the etheric (and so the physical) body of the receiver to improve their condition. Particularly so when the energized thought sent out is one of spiritual healing. If broadcasting can work on electronic laws then prayer can work on similar laws using a higher wavelength. The higher airwave frequencies known and used already by the angelic forces will be one day described by the scientists.

Having tried thus to analyse the practical working of healing prayers, I can hear some of my readers being offended. What right has this man to demean the God-given service of Divine

Intercession in this mundane manner? My reply is simple. The workings of the Divine Mind are immaculate. The workings of Science also. By the practical law of cause and effect, a miracle has to find a way of expressing itself. We are trying to examine this process of expression. Understanding how the divine and angelic forces are able to bring down their higher vibration of being to affect us on a lower plane in no way detracts from their splendour. Possibly the reverse. By looking at this mysterious and wonderful subject of Divine Intercession through the practical viewpoint of a non-believer, we might even inspire that non-believer to attribute the workings of science as originally coming from Divine Mind. Teilhard de Chardin, the French Jesuit, faced problems with the Roman church for thinking thus. But his courage and Divine inspiration kept him on course, so that his teaching is now realized as an enlightened bridgeway between faith and science. Like all truly universal minds he knew he was simply exploring another route through the Divine construction of the Cosmic Universe.

Jesus, we believe, spent a large part of his boyhood versed in the esoteric teaching of the Essenes, a sect who lived near Jerusalem. They understood and practised laws older than the church. They knew about the etheric body of man and about psychic energies, framed as their knowledge was in the religious beliefs of their sect. Jesus, being a Master containing a totally-evolved soul, knew about all these laws in his soul memory, but for the purposes of living out his particular mission in his earth life, he had chosen to go through the process of re-learning them. Thus he demonstrated the purpose of a life on planet Earth to inspire all lesser-evolved souls. Jesus had chosen to arrive through the usual channel of his mother's womb, albeit triggered into conception by a higher (or divine) energy. In living Jesus showed how physical laws can be overcome by his superb demonstration of the healing energy. So evolved was he that he could mould mud into two balls of matter which were translated by thought energy into perfectly-installed working eyes. He knew the etheric laws of cause and effect and demonstrated them. In telling us to love one another he was citing the positive use of constructive thought energy. Love is the greatest healer of all. Love works its miracles by setting into motion the eternal laws of positive action on a metaphysical level. It is possible that the boy Jesus travelled more widely than it is generally known to commune with other teachers than the Essenes to prepare himself for his final sacrifice. He was also preparing those teachers to leave behind a positive and energized level of knowledge which he knew would be needed to keep his teaching alive after his passing.

In dying Jesus demonstrated his greatest feat of all. Thoroughly versed in esoteric law, he raised the consciousness not only of his etheric body, the cradle of his soul, but he also raised the vibrations of his dead physical body and after re-energizing it with the power of spiritual life, he took that body with him as well. He chose to suffer his death to show us his torture to death at our hands was real. This was to teach us that we grow through suffering, and through change. When he showed himself later to Thomas and the others by temporarily lowering his vibrations to become visible on the human level, he did so to finish his earthly mission. He had arrived as a spirit in body, and he had left as transmuted body into spirit. The last showing in that particular chapter was to round off his practical demonstration of the etheric laws. It was all there for the beholder to learn. If he has shown himself in many guises to many people since, that is because his teaching work now is diffused on a wider level as is needed in this present age.

Although many good people talk about and await the Second Coming of Jesus to planet Earth as prophesied, it is possible, with respect, to interpret this in other ways. If we see man as having been given Divine Energy, then we can equally see man as reflecting the Godhead, in which case man can bring about the Second Coming collectively by raising his consciousness to thus reflect his divinity.

Jesus can manifest in all who thus attune.

The more we try to find out how spiritual healing works, the more we realize that all healing, whether achieved by allopathic or naturopathic means, by the laying on of hands or by prayer – or in some cases by a combination of several methods – is brought about by the resurgence of the life force. Some people view the switching on of the body's life force as 'mind over matter'. All doctors know that the patient's will to live can often save that patient, when the man in the next bed who lacks this drive often succumbs to his illness. It is also fair to say that the switching on of the body's life force – or life-saving force – is in itself a mystery. Similarly the use of certain drugs on certain symptoms brings a positive result which doctors welcome without being always able to analyse. There are other mysteries concerning the body and its life-saving force. Give a placebo (a false but harmless medicine) to ten people suffering from certain similar symptoms, and a certain percentage will improve. This can be as high as thirty percent of the patients who think the fake medicine has done them good – and so it has. The idea of taking it has regenerated their life-saving force. So 'mind over matter', as Coué knew, can never be underestimated. (Dr Coué was a French doctor who practised and taught this method of self-healing very successfully at the turn of the century.) On the other hand, a patient can benefit from healing prayers they may never acknowledge.

The body itself can unconsciously produce its own self-healing mechanism. Smash up a car's bodywork and it might take several skills to put it back into order. Certain damage to the human body including bruises, cuts, and much more, can be healed by the resources of the body alone. This can often be achieved without the extra stimulus of other treatment.

It has been known for some time that certain areas of the brain can produce their own deadening effect when needed. What the brain produces is an amino-acid known as an endorphine. A severely-wounded man often feels no immediate pain as a result of his brain instantly producing endorphine. Medical research in this area is finding further evidence about the body's capacity to produce other self-healing stimulators.

None of this ever-widening scientific knowledge takes away from the fact that the body's self-healing properties can not only be triggered off by the use of medical drugs but also by alternative therapies including spiritual healing. This latter method has several enormous advantages. Spiritual healing, to my knowledge, has never been known to harm. It can also be used from afar, an invisible power triggering off reactions in the etheric and so the physical body of the patient to re-kindle its wonderful self-healing properties.

In the writing of this chapter explaining how I think spiritual healing works, I am aware of my mortal limitations. If an important part of my particular sojourn on planet Earth is to demonstrate spiritual healing, it is also to learn and to share my knowledge. A teacher should be a few pages ahead of his pupils or further. Sometimes we learn from our pupils; and we are all students. Humility teaches me to always be aware of expanding knowledge. We must be ready to shed any notions we have which constrict us. Wisdom sometimes moves us to realize our human limitations and prejudices. The most beautiful of prayers I learned and spoke kneeling as a boy whilst my mother listened before tucking me into bed at night: 'Gentle Jesus meek and mild, look upon a little child, pity my simplicity, suffer me to come to Thee.' And so it is, and must be.

There may be readers who might think I have not sufficiently paid homage to the constant help and support I as a healer and a creative man receive from my friends, colleagues, co-workers and guides in spirit. As a medium who happens to have faith, I am made constantly and gratefully aware of our links with a higher world the source of all our inspiration. But over-insistence on this link can alienate many people who lead perfectly happy and satisfactory lives in every way unaware of the other dimension so close to them. Although several religions, indeed some of the foremost, contain the belief of acceptance of communion with higher and finer personalities placed above us in the Hierarchy, many people would not consider this essential to their well-being. I respect their opinion, as I would hope they respect mine. Nevertheless, in spite of our differences of attitude, they might, I trust, be interested to study the processes of spiritual healing, especially if it is presented with a non-sectarian or even a non-religious viewpoint.

It might well be, for reasons we do not yet fully understand concerning our evolvement as human and later as more highly-evolving souls, that we are supposed to see many things differently at this stage. It may be a necessary part of our development; I deeply suspect it is. Provided we are all proceeding as best we can towards the ultimate Truth, and providing we are using any knowledge we might glean to share with and help our fellow travellers, our route may be of secondary importance. More important might be the capacity to tear up our opinions in the light of newly-acquired knowledge and so to re-set our directing compass. The Truth can be approached by many routes, and be seen from many aspects. The essential is, after all, to keep moving, and to keep seeking, as we all attempt to aspire to the Ultimate.

9.
DOWN TO EARTH

IN this chapter I shall enlarge on various aspects of spiritual healing, the techniques I adopt, and further explanations of the emotions I experience whilst healing.

I am aware that some healers feel they are linked with one healing personality on a higher level who works through them. Others appear to work linked with several. Some are not conscious of being linked with any particular source of higher energies other than a general supply available to all who wish to tune in. In my case I feel at times all these emotions. Sometimes I link with one of my helpers in spirit, sometimes I am conscious of working with a group, and often I do my work without being especially conscious of any particular back up. Nevertheless whenever, after a moment's reflection, I look to my spiritual link, I know it is there and I know I do not work unsupported. Shall we say for long spaces of time I am trusted to get on with it. Provided I am giving the best possible help to my patient that I can offer, I do not question the workings, but simply ask to be used to relay the higher forces of healing power down to earth. My head chakra receives the etheric energy and I am the medium to convey it through my etheric body and out of my hands. Provided I place myself at the right time in the right place having tuned in, the quality of the healing is also out of my hands. As the patient has put their trust in me, so I put my trust in the higher realms. That is what spiritual healing is about.

If whilst writing and talking about spiritual healing I refer to the sick who come to me in person for help, or who write to me for help from a distance (absent or distant healing) it is because this is the simplest way of referring to them. I in no way use the word 'patient' to suggest I am a doctor – spiritual or psychic therapist would be more accurate. As we healers give the laying on of hands as taught by Jesus, some refer to their healing work as a ministry. I refer to myself either as a healer or as a spiritual or psychic healer.

Of course I am aware sometimes whilst healing of the presence of a personality, some of which the reader will have met. My linking up with the warm and powerful Brave Spirit is an event which marked my spiritual development. Not that I claim to see or hear from him every time I give healing. Far from it. But, neither does that mean we are far from each other on a prayer or spiritual level. We have plenty of friends on planet Earth that we might not contact regularly for a host of reasons. But if they are true friends they understand our silences and they continue to give out their friendship towards us. This is something we can feel, enjoy, and hopefully reciprocate. So it is with our spiritual helpers. We are grateful for their being and the knowledge of their link with us. When, on the other hand, I call for help, they send it. 'Ask and ye shall receive' is a cosmic law. The help may not come in the way we would immediately choose, but often it does. It always comes to us in the way we can most benefit. There are times we have to apparently struggle on alone. These moments are needed to strengthen us. Only strong people can stand alone. It is one of the hardest lessons to learn. When we have learned it we are of more value to our fellow man and no doubt to our spiritual links.

Endless introspection into the processes of mediumship is unwise. Once a person has discovered how to use his mediumship for a useful purpose, it is better to do just that. The energy used in wondering how it works is, for the average medium, better placed in the work itself. That is, after all, hard enough to get right.

Psychic work should be undertaken only by the psychically strong. The healer must attend to his health first before he is ready to be the channel for the healing forces to be shared with others. More thoughts on this point later.

I am happy to feel that in my healing ministry I receive help and energy from more than one spiritual personality. I was made aware of this some years ago when the patient before me, who happened to be my milkman at the time, suffering from an ear problem, was seated in my healing chair. As I tuned in to ask for help for him, a spiritual doctor impressed his presence on me. He showed up with a shock of red hair, his white house-doctor's hospital coat, and a strong Scottish accent. Telling me he had been killed in a car smash, still in his thirties, on the motorway leading north, he set speedily to work on my patient. His hands seem to move about at double speed as he examined and gave healing to my – now our – patient. As soon as the work was done, my doctor visitor vanished. I sent my thanks afterwards when I learned that our patient, naturally unaware of my spirit collaborator, received great benefit from the healing. I have seen and had help from this doctor since, but his visits are rare. He has other work to do.

Healing Technique

To enlarge on my previous remarks about my healing technique, I emphasize that my personal aim is simplicity.

In the ordinary event I give healing by appointment. This enables me to prepare myself and to limit the number of people I can receive in one healing session. I see people separately, and I limit my healing work to certain times on certain days. Although the healing power is given to flow through me, I naturally use up a lot of my own energy in receiving the patient, listening to their story, and after the healing bidding them farewell. Sometimes the perimeters of the work are more tiring than the work itself. Listening to the patient's tale of woe is often of great importance. One is sharing their load. Sometimes people have travelled far and waited long to see me. I respect this also.

Having arranged a certain healing session, I prepare myself accordingly. Whether I am sitting quietly in my sanctuary, doing a little quiet weeding in the garden, or playing the piano, I am also going through the motions of raising my consciousness to prepare myself for the healing session. Kneeling in prayer is not necessary to me as a technique for raising my consciousness, nor is it to be avoided. As explained in the section on brain rhythms I am one of those people who can be doing practical things whilst tuning in and up. Nevertheless by preference I choose only certain activities before healing and I like to be more or less quiet. I am fully aware of the responsibility of my healing commitments, but I do not carry it as a burden.

Once I have received my patient and often their companion I usually sit them on my piano stool, a convenient place to have access to their spinal column. The listening to their story has already taken place in a chair with a back. Once they are on the stool, more often than not I explore, as it were, their aura. I place my hands about their head and spine with very gentle stroking movements. As I tune into their presence, I often receive impressions about their physical, mental and psychic state. Sometimes I discover things about them which they have not chosen to tell me, and sometimes not. Whatever takes place, I have to decide whether it is wise to share my new-found knowledge with them or not. This depends sometimes on how they have answered the question I nearly always put to them, 'Have you seen your doctor?'

If this question surprises them, or the reader, remember all information concerning the patient is important. No healer of value should come between his patient and any medical treatment he might be undertaking. Spiritual healing runs alongside any other treatment. Sometimes, of course, we are the last resort, the doctors having failed, alas, to help. If I should not ask the patient if they have seen a doctor it would be because from one source or another I had already been briefed about them.

I make no claim to diagnosis. That does not mean that I cannot often sense a problem with a patient. Sometimes the knowledge seems to fall into my mind, sometimes I hear it on my clairaudience, and sometimes I seem to be shown diagrams which can instantly alert me to the presence of illness of a particular nature or form. As I use my hands to relay the healing forces I am often drawn to place them on a particular place, causing the patient to say, 'You've found the place.'

As already stated, they may feel heat or cold coming from my hands or one or the other of them. Sometimes they feel a sensation like pins and needles flowing down the blocked energy line as it is being treated by the healing energies. Sometimes, as in the case of Joanna Syms (see chapter one) physical changes take place which involve some actual physical sounds. During this process no discomfort is experienced by my patient. Sometimes I start the process of healing which might be continued later. I have witnessed the freeing of a moving part of the body which has been previously causing trouble, as the patient starts to leave the healing sanctuary. This is probably the most mysterious aspect of the process of healing which I have had to accept. Sometimes no apparent help is given to the patient at the time of the laying on of hands, but it might manifest, hours, days, and even months later. I never question the method; I accept that the corrective work has to be done thus, before the result can be brought about. Some change obviously has to be put in motion in the patient before the healing is made apparent. However long it will be my destiny to be a healer in this life on planet Earth, I could never be blasé about the work. I keep the same sense of wonder about it today as when I started accepting my healing talent all those years ago.

Many patients feel sleepy during, after, or even before healing whilst in my presence. Once I have raised my consciousness the healing energies summoned to vibrate about me undoubtedly cast their spell. I speak of this particularly because I have to warn those driving to see me to deal with this effect sensibly. I often advise them to rest before driving far.

One of my patients had always to be driven straight home by her accompanying husband and placed onto a couch. For a good three-quarters of an hour she would then rest in a perfectly relaxed and happy state but apparently unwilling or even, it seems, unable to move. She received, in fact, dramatic release from diverticulitis which had plagued her for over twenty years, to the point of her having to receive morphia, such was the pain, and having to lose her profitable work more than once. If the result of healing took its special and immediate effect on her, it was worth it. After years of having to eat what was virtually baby food, she rang me shortly after her third healing session to say, 'I've just eaten roast pork and all the trimmings, I feel fine, and I can hardly believe my luck after over twenty years of my boring enforced diet.'

Her husband, my patient and I all rejoiced together. It was he who said a short time later, 'Thank you for handing me back my wife as she was those years ago.'

Sometimes whilst healing, perhaps more so in the early days, I am shown a detailed close-up of a part of some inner organ of the patient to study. One particular patient I remember had an inflammation in his stomach which I saw as crimson and uneven. Sensing the beginnings of an ulcer, I gave him the advice a friend might know, such as not to go hungry, eat little and often, cut out the frying pan and drink milk with honey. After his second healing session he was fast recovering.

More often than not I might sense the patient's problems,

rather than seeing them. Usually they tell me about their symptoms. Very occasionally I glean facts which I am asked by my spirit helpers not to divulge to the patient as they might not be ready to accept them.

I am sometimes asked what percentage of patients get better. This is probably the most difficult question to answer. A lot of people contact me for help whom I might never hear from again. Sometimes they write years later, saying that they were healed by me x years before and that now they have come back with a different problem or for help for someone else. It would be wrong to be upset by their apparent lack of interest in informing me about their previous positive experience, but we are only human and it naturally gives me great joy to hear of a patient's recovery. Sometimes I fear for those whose apparent indifference might lead them somehow back into illness. We do, I am sure, control our health to a great degree, and the emotional pattern which can lead us to disease might well lead us back to it, should we not correct our attitudes or life pattern.

Some of us need illness as part of our soul education. It teaches us a lot.

According to Dr Alec Forbes, a doctor turned healer who founded the Bristol clinic, all competent therapists of whatever accepted variety, provided they are qualified, bring about roughly the same results in terms of success or failure rates; that is, one third get better, one third find improvement, and one third cannot be helped by that particular treatment. I would not like personally to be quoted as having given any figures at this moment in time. Spiritual healing is such a wonderful and various force of good, that it sometimes works variously and wonderfully through many avenues and levels of consciousness. It might well be beyond being contained by statistics.

Life-Giving Habits for Healers

I personally like to keep to a reasonable body weight. If weight needs to be lost, or diet routines and intake studied, I would always advise consulting a qualified dietician and/or a doctor.

I choose not to eat a large meal before giving healing, nor do I choose to be hungry. Personally over-intake of nicotine or alcohol is disadvantageous to the smooth working of my psychic senses. I am well aware that my physical body houses my spiritual, and that I must keep a good balance of exercise, sleep, food intake and meditation to be the best possible instrument I can offer for the use as a healer by the higher forces. I am allowed a full life as a human being, but as a healer I must keep a reasonable balance. As a psychic and healer my position is special in that I am my own instrument. Like so many singers, athletes and dancers we have to submit to certain disciplines to fulfil our potential.

It has been my particular destiny to have started my healing work with my own body. This gives me the special responsibility of being in a way my own product. I do not think the patients who come to me for help would have confidence if they found a man falling apart at the seams. I do know there are healers who do good work who happen to suffer infirmities of many kinds. That too is their destiny. Mine is to try to inspire in others the on-going healthy path that I have been inspired to take. The years bring all sorts of challenges to us all, but I try to meet them with my intrinsic desire to sustain the self-healing forces within my body, so as to be of use to others.

I was fortunate to have been encouraged as a young man to find a way through to health, and a desire to sustain it. I have mentioned the German doctor who taught me so many basic rules of diet and exercise. Another early influence on my interest in sustaining health came upon me in Paris. 'If you are lucky enough to have lived in Paris as a young man, then wherever you go for the rest of your life it stays with you, for Paris is a movable feast,' wrote Ernest Hemingway to a friend in 1950. I am one of those lucky men.

One of the many ingredients of my particular movable feast was coming across the writings, and under the influence, of a famous American dietician called Gaylord Hauser. This man made a great career for himself, writing, lecturing and supplying information and products concerning diet, food additives, aspects of nutrition and the care of the body and so the mind. He occasionally called in to our apartment in the rue de Seine and although my visits never coincided with his, I came across his traces on the kitchen shelf. He had kindly left us vitamins and other food additives to boost us against the Paris winter in our fairly primitive but colourful conditions on the Left Bank.

Gaylord Hauser was the man who gave dietetic advice to thousands of people including Greta Garbo. I studied every book of his I could lay my hands on in the local library on my return to England. I remember one of his great adages is always start and finish a meal with something raw. He put me onto wonderful recipes using every kind of raw food and the use of molasses and also of brewer's yeast. My neighbours in Brighton grew accustomed to strongly-smelling packets of brewer's yeast which I had delivered straight from the brewery.

Hauser's tips on the use of sitz baths have refreshed me on many an occasion in my travels. This technique is basically the splashing about of cold or warm water whilst squatting in any container large enough, from a bath to a shower enclosure, etc. Ideally this should take place with clean water after washing. It is a different concept of refreshing the body, other than lying in a warm, soapy bath, which of course has other functions and advantages.

I was extremely lucky to have found these health tips as a young man. People are always stressing the importance of getting your body and diet in order when you pass forty. I consider this is ten years too late to make the task easy. Thirty to me is the watershed age. A person should be taught to be organized in their exercise, food and life habits by then. Otherwise the fight later to battle with middle age spread can be much harder, although nowadays there is much more help available in terms of diet, exercise programmes and therapies.

Meeting Judy Garland in Paris during that period was a reminder of the importance of keeping the body in good shape. A friend of ours was presenting her in her one woman show after a long spell of private and career problems. The great days of Hollywood were already behind her, the many films she had made to dazzle us with her many-sided talents as singer, dancer and actress were long ago registered on celluloid for all time. Judy, now a plump, mature woman with her curiously short neck and much widened waist, was quite a shock to meet after my memories of her early self partnering Mickey Rooney or Fred Astaire in those enchanting musicals. As I shook her gloved hand on the corner of the Boulevard St Germain I was greeted with an explosive smile and a 'How do you do?' which made me forget her problems. I could see the great star energy still there, and those dark eyes shone enough for all of us.

On stage at the vast Palais de Chaillot a few days later Judy bounced on, her famous legs looking great and her welcome making up for the plump frame decorated in yards of black net and sequins exploding about her as if she had stepped out of half a cracker. After a few words in halting French and rather faltering American one realized, after the huge welcome had died down, that she was not only nervous, she was semi-frozen with panic. Old stager that she was, Miss Garland moved about from centre stage to side stage pretending to arrange the trailing cord of her hand microphone to her advantage. She made it twirl and coil like a cobra, a feat which drew a laugh of nervous relief from the audience. When she asked for and got a 'slug of water' her hand trembled as she drank what we all suspected was not that at all. Thus braced, she attacked the centre of the stage once more, the orchestra leader doing his best to lead her into her first number. But nothing was forthcoming. It was then that I saw a perfect example of what was in its way spiritual healing.

Maurice Chevalier was singled out by Judy, who had spotted him in the front row. He bowed to us and then, realizing as a fellow artist that Judy Garland was having problems, he did a wonderful thing. Taking the red carnation from the lapel of his dinner jacket he kissed it and threw it up for her to catch. '*Chante pour moi*,' he called out. 'Sing for me.'

That did it. With a somewhat faltering voice she launched into her first number, and by the third she was truly warmed up and in her roof-raising stride. She belted out *The Trolley Song* until the whole audience and the vast stadium were seemingly on wheels. In spite of the plump waist, her Parisian comeback was a triumph. Chevalier's healing gesture had worked, and we all bathed in her personal sunshine.

When some years later I met Judy Garland again, the contrast was dramatic. Personal problems and prescribed drugs were driving the life force out of this remarkable woman. I was accompanying Hermione Baddeley to a London first night, a Lionel Bart musical, where we met Noël Coward* in the bar at interval time. Coward was accompanying Judy Garland. Her now pencil-thin form in a skin-tight creation of pink shading to red with artificial shell-like beads which showed a scarlet heart motif in place, she looked in one way superb, in another perilous. As I looked at her drawn face heavily painted under that defiant quiff of black hair my inner eye saw a woman half

---

* Now Sir Noël Coward.

wanting to leave the fight. Noël Coward in his witty and urbane way had leant Judy against the wall, tottering as she was on elegant scarlet shoes, her thin legs just visible through a slit in her skirt enabling her to walk – except that she couldn't quite. Coward expertly guided her back to her centre stalls seat as the lights were fading after the interval, so that as few as possible would realize the state of his partner. At the party afterwards, Garland leant against the white piano but waved away her musical introduction. She had already gone over the rainbow – into a living nightmare. When, some time later, I heard the news flash that she was gone, I felt saddened and relieved. I sent a prayer of thanks for all the joy she had brought this world, and I am certain now, to the next.

Watching Liza Minelli recently perform her one-woman show, demonstrating her own considerable individual talents, I was aware in some of her back-throat trilling notes of her mother's heritage. I was also aware that Minelli fought so well her battle against drugs and alcohol which would have destroyed her career as it did finally her mother's. As a man who spends a lot of time and energy healing, praying and writing about encouraging and sustaining the life force, may I be allowed to say well done to you, Miss Minelli. Your example must have inspired many to do likewise. Should you ever get to read this page, may I tell you something I suspect you already know. Your wonderful mother was with you in spirit every inch of that tough fight to dry out. Continue please, mother and daughter, to let us enjoy memories past, and memories future.

If in these pages about spiritual healing you expected to find a book which would only instruct a chosen few so-called believers in how to raise your vibrations to bring about a better balance of your mind, body and spirit, by now you will have been disillusioned. Prayer, energy, personal life force linking with Cosmic Energy, all these subjects and more are not merely for the cloistered few, they are for everyone. True, I have by my destiny to spend a long time in meditation and a state of raised consciousness for my healing work. But my chosen life-style can and does bring me into contact with people whose lives are as widely contrasting as one could imagine. If one moment I am sharing my notes on prayer and in the next describing the dress Judy Garland wore, I offer no apologies. After all, to steal a metaphor from a song-writing genius, 'a spoonful of sugar makes the medicine go down'. Life was never meant to be a conventional, stereotyped affair impressing on us that work is a bore and that we have to conform to this tradition or that with our spare energies. Providing we are using our life force constructively, provided we are obeying the great eternal law of cause and effect with all the responsibility that that puts upon us to love our fellow man, then we are allowed to break many so-called attitudes. Some of the best prayer can take place, after all, outside a church as well as within it. If meeting world-famous names gives us a lift, and the chance to share that moment with many others – how can that be wrong? All work looks easy if it's well done. Everybody else's life looks easier and more glamorous until you really get to know the people involved. We work and we pay for everything. Nothing is for free except Cosmic Energy.

As I write this in my hide-away in St Tropez, a hibiscus flower shows its superb design, placed in a glass of water on my writing table. I nurtured the plant on my balcony, warmed by the Mediterranean sun of this autumn. I am forever grateful that I had the courage those years ago to buy my tiny home here perched on high as it is with its glimpse of the harbour. If I paid for it with the fruits of theatre work, it has re-paid me with many a holiday. Armed with my type-writer I arrive for the health-giving sun and the chance to swim much later in the year than in the colder northern seas. The wonderful selection of vegetables from the local market encourages me to be more adventurous with my cooking. The occasional entertaining of my friends is a great joy, though living in one studio room has its problems – book pages have to be tidied up to make way for plates of home-cooked pasta and reference notes are liable to get tangled up in the serviettes. But I do not envy my rich friends with their elegant villas and their swimming pools. Villas need servants to clean them, pools have to be constantly cleaned out and fussed over. I have the blue-green Mediterranean waters to swim in. I can think of Colette as I swim at her favourite beach of Les Salins with its coral-coloured sand and its nearby noble pine parasol trees. As I jog on the shore, the sky is my roof, I feel as free as the wind which causes the sea to dance and spray its surf like the beaten white of egg. Standing on the wild rocks which frame the shore my healing prayers can wing their way around the world.

Drug Addiction

I have already discussed the situation Judy Garland found herself in after severe problems with prescribed drugs. It is no secret that the studio system in those days put her as a child star on prescribed drugs to manipulate her energies for the most efficient work schedule. Drugs to wake up and drugs to sleep were administered with the disastrous results which followed. Such a programme would not, of course be allowed today since we have learned the dangers of such over-use of drugs and the consequences. But we had to learn.

Millions of people today find themselves addicted to medically prescribed drugs, usually so-called tranquillizers which were given them in all faith by doctors following the teaching and the way of thinking of the day. An over-worked doctor only able to give a few minutes to each patient might have been pleased to use these once-praised tranquillizers to help the suffering of his patients with symptoms ranging from stress and insomnia to forms of depression. A stroke of the pen on a prescription form came as a blessed relief to both the patient and the doctor. Now, in some cases irreversible physical and nervous symptoms have manifested in vast numbers of people who have struggled and sometimes failed to come off the drugs after years of what develops into addiction. The doctors of today are of course alerted to this problem and a different attitude is abroad. Both the medical authorities and the patients realize that society was using the newly-found drugs to an exaggerated degree. Certain drugs are of course highly-efficient tools to cure or ease many symptoms. But in terms of the use of tranquillizers, the present day mood is to be much more cautious in their use. We have learned our lesson.

Spiritual healing has played its full part as an aid to people wanting to come off tranquillizers. I have helped many people gradually step off the tranquillizer roundabout. Sometimes the process has to be long and gradual. But the coming back to full life of the freed patient is wonderful to behold.

As for the ever-growing modern phenomena of social drug addiction, that is quite another problem. Having only been invited to try to help a very limited number of people to kick the drug-taking habit, I am not qualified to make much comment. One girl I did help over quite a long period, years rather than months, managed, with help from several directions, to emerge from her nightmare back into life. She is now happily married with several bouncing children and works in the probation service. With her experience she is a valued worker. The troubled will always respond better to those they sense instinctively have known trouble themselves. Genuine compassion and personal experience must be the most valuable requisites for any social worker.

If I am asked today to offer help to social drug-addicted people, I usually refer them to clinics and groups working solely in this area of rescue.

Alcoholics

Although I might be able to encourage an alcoholic to come off the miserable roundabout of excess, hangover and remorse, generally speaking I refer them to Alcoholics Anonymous, a wonderful organization with branches all over the country. Here the alcoholic meets with his fellow sufferer and together they go to work to crack the problem. Relapses are many, but once a person has taken the great step of realizing they have a drink problem and taken the decision to fight it, the presence of an organized group of other sufferers about them is of enormous help.

One of the problems of any addiction is the personality change brought about by the craving and the moral destruction which can follow. Hitherto honest, decent people can become lying monsters when addicted. Once the personality breaks down, the person is open to attack by dark forces which can literally black out the former light of the person concerned. Addiction is far more than a physical problem, it becomes a psychic problem. In terms of drug addiction, a lot of the rising rate of violent crime can be attributed to it. People will steal, beat up and murder for a drug fix. Alcoholics have been known to do the same. I would hate to have the job of trying to bring forth a practical solution to the present vast number of youngsters fighting for their lives to escape from drug addiction and alcoholism. The use of positive mental energy projected towards them and encouraged within them must have a helpful effect. If the word prayer switches them off, then other words should be used in talking about this energy potential which we can generate for ourselves or for our fellow men. A group of people fighting a problem must surely always be stronger than the loneliness of individual or person-to-person struggling. As I write this I send out my prayer energy to ask for help and inspiration to all those helping the addicted, and to the addicted themselves for strength to fight their way out of their private hell. There, but for the grace of God, could go any of us.

Speaking personally, I was lucky enough to have been a youngster before the widespread fashion of teenage drug experimenting started. Drugs were not about. As for alcohol, it was always available at home and one learned to enjoy it and use it with respect, a pattern I have luckily been able to follow ever since. As a healer I work for health, never against it.

Other Addictions

Gambling fever is a very real addiction where surely healing prayers could not be wasted. Again I refer people to the groups in existence to help those addicted to try to break their down-spiral pattern. Many children and older people become addicted to the machines, commonly referred to as one-arm bandits, available in certain establishments. As with so many addictions, a little I suppose can be fun, and beyond that problems can start. That last remark does not apply to drugs, because in my opinion it would be irresponsible of me to write one word encouraging any social drug-taking. I realize each generation has its tools of relaxation, but in my estimation I would rather see someone having a little alcohol to relax them than a little social drug. I am fully aware that there are thousands of people who use certain drugs to relax them, saying it does them no harm. As a healer I would not like to enter into this trap of recommendation. I would prefer to work for their well-being and leave each individual depending on his age, work, state of health and finances to find his own solution to these very important problems.

I note with interest that whenever the word 'addiction' comes up we all tend to end up voicing once more our opinions on drug-taking, for we all know it is one of the greatest problems which modern society faces. Again I say that perhaps I am better qualified to stand back and get on with my healing.

The Need for Love

Reliance on alcohol, drugs, and other forms of escape is often triggered off by a lack of love. All human beings need someone or something to love, and in turn to be loved by someone or something. We know that the animal kingdom plays its great part here in supplying companionship to man. How many people will tell you their lives would be empty but for their pet animal as companion? More about this later.

Some people in their craving for love will, consciously or more usually unconsciously, reach out for illness to supply their desire for care and love. A well person does not get the same treatment from society as a sick one. I reckon a proportion of those people we see being wheeled about in a wheel-chair have long realized they can get total attention from another human being by becoming physically dependent on them.

On the other hand there are also those people who need to have someone to cosset and fuss over. Apart from the dedicated nurses and others whose professional work is to care for the sick there are others who need an invalid to look after as fulfilment. I suppose it is the law of supply and demand. Some need to be cosseted, some need to cosset.

A woman I once knew cared for a sick man who eventually became a wheel-chair case. She took him on luxury cruises. Once at a party given for him in France I was by chance alone, the other guests having moved through to the food in a neighbouring room, leaving me with the invalid. I know he was a very sick man, but I also know that, thinking he was unobserved, he rose from his habitual position in his wheel-chair and quite casually poured himself a glass of champagne. That tiny incident taught me a great deal about the almost desperate need of some people to be loved. Sometimes it can be stronger than the desire to overcome an illness.

I knew too of a woman who invented illnesses to become operated upon. Her list of successes was awesome. She apparently fooled specialist after specialist and achieved a wide variety of operations, many or all I suspect totally unnecessary. Her need for love was expressed in a bizarre desire to be examined, handled and operated upon. A good love mate earlier in her life might have saved the health service a small fortune.

Sometimes, although a sick person knows that by using huge

concentration over a certain period that they have the power within them to unlock and release themselves from an illness, mental and/or physical, yet they do not carry this through. They may be lazy. It can be easier and more desirable for some to lie back and stay poorly than to stand up (mentally or physically) and fight. They choose to luxuriate in the negativity of acceptance, enjoying the power it may bring them over others. Whatever the reason, action is life. Immobility is death. If we voluntarily fail to encourage and use the precious life-force available, we are switching ourselves off from progressing in a negative gesture of ingratitude. Somewhere along the line of our future soul history we will be roused and inspired to reverse our negative attitudes. Wherever possible or necessary, why not start thinking and acting positively now? Try it, you will be surprised at the result.

The results of health coming back to a sick partner can be just as devastating as the reverse. A lady patient of mine, released from debilitating and physically and mentally constricting pain now presents, with her new freedom, a different challenge to her loving husband. Smothered by years of family illness including her own, this woman is now travelling widely and following the long pent-up urge to free herself from her partner. Wisely he has left the door open. The person who may return is already a different one – more fulfilled, more valuable.

Emotional Detachment

All therapists have to learn emotional independence from their patients. Spiritual or psychic healers also. In no way am I telling healers to be less compassionate, but one has to be both psychically linked with the patient whilst attempting to help them, and then remain part observer. If I were to forge an emotional link with each sick person I treat I would not be able to continue healing. As a human being it is only natural that certain cases might touch me more than others. One is perhaps more liable to be touched by the problems of, for example, a very young and sick child. But one has to remember that the best healing work is done in a state of raised consciousness and not wallowing in a morass of pity. If I have been given a high sensitivity which enables me to respond to the needs of others, I have to learn to protect that sensitivity and not abuse it. Steering a middle path between caring and acting on this compassion, takes practice. But possibly only then can healers do their best work. Energy must be kept for the giving of healing, not eroded by needlessly stressing the negative elements of the situation. Healers have to learn to translate the disharmony of disease into the harmony of health with the least possible fuss. Concentration on the positive is everything. Energy must be saved for that.

Energy

It cannot be stressed too often that the healer's energy must be kept topped up. Although Cosmic Energy flowing through the instrument, which is the healer's etheric apparatus, is of capital importance, his own energy must also be involved. A regular exercise and sleep pattern is certainly needed for this healer, and I would judge for others. All human beings with work to do need regular relaxation, sport and/or hobbies to achieve this. Remember too that fresh food is not only full of nutrients, it is also vibrating with the life force. Look at the energetic pattern of vibrations given out by a fresh lettuce leaf or a newly-baked piece of bread as seen by the Kirlian method of examination, then compare this with a stale example of both, and you will be convinced about the difference of energy value in fresh food. Deep-freezing of food is enormously practical and is used in varying degrees by most of us. But to receive maximum energy from any diet there is nothing better than including fresh products.

Certain people are energy vampires. We have to learn to discern them and combat their desire to drain us of psychic energy. The telephone is a weapon they like to use. I have learned to limit my conversations with the sick to a minimum if I am to be of best service to them. Hooking them up to absent healing is one thing, draining oneself of energy listening to their endless stream of negative news is another. Personal exposure to the neurotic has to be carefully rationed if the healer is to remain buoyant for his everyday healing work. Vampires come in many forms.

In the next chapter I will continue to discuss various aspects of healing from the point of view of both the healer and the patient.

10.
MORE ASPECTS OF HEALING

What Types of Illness Respond to Spiritual Healing?

PEOPLE who have generally not taken the trouble to do any research on the subject love to generalize by saying that only psychosomatic illness responds to spiritual healing. The inference being that as, in their opinion, psychosomatic illness is not a real illness, but only a false illness dreamed up by the conscious or the sub-conscious mind of the patient, the healing of it is also imaginary.

First it must be said that psychosomatic illness can bring about symptoms of a very real nature. Secondly it must be added that you cannot put a limit on the power of spiritual healing nor can you list diseases that it can or cannot help to fight. If you say it cannot help a man who has lost his leg by accident or by surgery, you might be wrong. Spiritual healing can help the patient recover from surgery, readjust to crisis and move forward into new problems with confidence and better general health.

When I look into my testimony file I find many such stories. There was a young man, for example, who crashed his motor-bike, and had severe physical problems after hospitalization. The deep depression which would have held back his recovery was removed almost immediately by absent healing, with the result that although the doctors said he might be in bed for months, and probably unable to take the examination for which he had been preparing himself, he proved them wrong on both counts. Leaving hospital within a short time, he took his exam and passed it. Within months he was back playing sport and getting on with his life. He was engaged and then married soon afterwards. It was as if the healing switched his attitude from negative to positive concerning his situation and allowed his body to switch on its self-healing capacities to the fullest extent.

When his uncle suffered severe cardiac attacks, he too amazed everyone by recovering from a highly precarious health condition, survived by-pass surgery, and came back to the remarkably good health he is still enjoying about a decade later. His family knows that healing helped him.

The list of ailments and conditions which I have seen healing help is long and growing longer. If it has been my lot to have helped people recover recently from some severe and chronic back problems, that may be by chance. I would not like to say these cases were my speciality, by a long way.

What I would like to say always is that I never claim to cure any disease or condition or even help it before the event. I simply start the healing, when invited to, either distant or contact or both, and I let matters take their course. I await to see to what degree healing helps the patient, or not, with as much interest as they do. One thing I have learned is never to limit the power of spiritual healing. If I were to, I would not be a healer. For surely the whole process is activated by that very assumption. You can therefore see it would be as useless to draw up a list of conditions that the power of healing can help, as it would be to draw up a list of the conditions it cannot help. The proof of the healing is in the healing.

The other welcome thought about healing is this. As it can help motivate the body to heal itself, so I feel sure it can also encourage the body's built-in immune system. Healing linked with meditation can help the body to stay well. Spiritual healing is never wasted, and knows no limits in its progress towards positive health and well-being. A fulfilled soul and mind will always choose to live in a healthy and fulfilled body.

Depression

Nearly every one of us, if we are to be honest, has experienced and/or does experience times when we feel depressed to a greater or lesser degree.

If we think out the situation in which we find ourselves, there is more often than not a valid reason for our mood. If by action we can change the immediate circumstance often we can also clear the depression. Not always. On the other hand sometimes life hands us one or a series of blows which might not make us depressed at all. Acceptance of the inevitable is sometimes the recipe to keep mentally buoyant. Meditation is a splendid technique for self-release from the negative effect of depression. More of this technique later.

Clinical depression is of another order. Once the patient succumbs, their situation requires diagnosis to understand. No amount of the usual remedies releases them. If a cup of tea, or a walk, or a chat, even with a stranger, can often lift a temporary dark mood, clinical depression is something else. The person suffering is totally in a mood of despair. Often this can lead to self-destruction, and self-destruction can be achieved in a thousand ways. Once the life force ceases to flow, the body can start to refuse food and the mind refuse attempts at being helped. Suicide takes many forms.

Though allopathic medicine can offer much hope with drug treatment, we have already discussed the risk of dependency which can follow. Electric-shock therapy has helped many, but there can be problems such as post-therapy memory erosion. In severe cases the treatment might have to be resumed after periodical relapse. Clinical depression can be a hard nut to crack. Spiritual healing is a very useful weapon.

I have already cited the case of Pauline Lennon who came to me originally suffering from depression, and the happy outcome of the change in her life after spiritual healing. Another more recent case was that of a young man called Andrew. He was brought to me by his mother, a community nurse who had previously received great help in recovering from an operation for a tumour of the brain. It was I who urged Peggy to go to hospital to be examined for a tumour which I sensed needed immediate surgery. This being the case, Peggy was operated on very shortly afterwards with the result that she had considerable problems with the use of her legs after surgery. After a rather dismal prognosis and recommendation of a long course of physiotherapy before she might be able to resume work, she contacted me again for absent healing. Within a short time Peggy was totally fit and had resumed full-time work as a nurse, a situation which still holds today, several years later.

One year after her own healing, Peggy brought me her son,

Andrew, who along with other problems was suffering from depression.

When Andrew was ushered into my healing room by his mother I was faced with a real challenge. Barely wanting to mutter more than a minimal greeting, Andrew sat on my piano stool, head bowed, looking, with his dark uncontrolled hair and neglected appearance, like a half-drowned starling. I explained to him that I was going to try to change his brain rhythms with the energy which flowed from my hands when needed. I thought this simple explanation might appeal to him as a young lad. His apparently total disinterest did not raise my hopes of being able to help him. It also made me try the harder. As I raised my consciousness to the highest possible level I could achieve I gave him the laying on of hands about his head. There was a very long silence lasting several minutes. I will never forget what followed. Tentatively I put the question to him, 'How are you, Andrew?'

There followed a second's pause before he answered, still head down, 'Great.'

Trying not to appear over-anxious I repeated the question. This time Andrew lifted up his head to show a calm expression as he repeated, 'I feel great.'

Spiritual healing had lifted him completely out of depression in a matter of minutes. If only every case of depression were as easy. Months of previous drug treatment for Andrew had failed. Visits to a psychiatric hospital had hardly helped him. His anger, expressed with certain violence against society, had resulted in trouble with the police and a life of restriction. Within a few days Andrew had seen to a new haircut, new clothes and a totally new way of life. He was keen to throw his prescribed drugs down the lavatory after telling his doctor he was well.

The latest news I received of Andrew fairly recently confirmed his enjoyment of a totally new life. His nightmare was ended and the world was before him. Such is the power of spiritual healing.

STRESS

Stress, like food additives of every sort and exposure to air, land and sea pollution, is one of the hazards of modern life. Curiously enough, a little stress can be beneficial in that it stimulates us into action, making the body produce adrenalin for example, a substance which activates. Many a person has saved their own life and those of others, fired, as it were, by stress. But stress can also kill. Over a longer rather than a shorter period it can cause the body and the mind sometimes irreparable damage. Stress can lead to high blood-pressure, gastric ulcers, rheumatoid arthritis, asthma, and countless other symptoms bringing illness and finally the running down of the life force slowly or quickly through, for example, cardiac failure or cerebral haemorrhage.

If I have cited some of the more dramatic physical possibilities due to stress, remember too it can erode the balanced working of the nervous system. Stress can and often does lead to a complete nervous breakdown and all the problems which ensue. It can lead to other nervous illness as well.

Vivien Leigh was an example of how stress over a long period can erode the nervous system and allow other problems to manifest. I once wished I had met her when I was a more experienced healer, for I could possibly have been of more help to her. But destiny works out its own pattern.

As I am so often asked my opinion on destiny and free will, I shall take this opportunity to briefly give my reply. Imagine an individually-made pot on a shelf, and within it place a dried pea. The pot is your destiny, the pea is you. We have the capacity, with determination and hard work, to make the pea swell up and fill the pot, or only partly fill it should we give up the struggle. We cannot change the shape and size of the pot, but we can, with a lot of effort, fill it right up. I cannot change my pot and become Beethoven, for example, but if I work hard I can fill out the possibilities of my life as Allon Bacon. So with every one of us, we are given our pot of destiny and the free will to fulfil it.

A lot of illness comes as a personal challenge which we are often allowed to overcome, partly or completely. Illnesses caused by stress, which are legion, encourage me to treat stress as a major health hazard. People working in areas of high stress have to learn to deal with it, or go under.

My mother was another example of someone who could not, for one reason or another, deal with the mounting stress she had to face.

A third case of stress, this example being one that I treated successfully, was, as it happens, a man. He too was working in the stressful world of show-business. My meeting with him was prefaced by my meeting with the international star of great talent, Charlotte Rampling.

Invited to a party by the French screen and stage actress Anne Vernon, I found myself in one of two buildings which sat together as a part of an old hamlet situated at the end of a long valley inland from Cogolin, a market town a few kilometres in the country beyond St Tropez. Anne Vernon, having relinquished her career as an actress (she acted in *The Umbrellas of Cherbourg*, shown world-wide), was now producing naïve paintings at a great rate. She was also very interested in the psychic world, hence my presence at the party.

Sitting as I was on the floor, imagine my surprise and pleasure when Charlotte Rampling walked in with two friends and because of space sat next to me. It is always interesting to meet stars one has seen magnified into huge close-ups on the silver screen. Miss Rampling offered no disappointment, with her finely carved face, her lynx-like grey-blue eyes and that long brown hair falling loosely over a slim figure wearing blue jeans and a simple form-fitting top. Curiously enough, as we got chatting, I received a message which I gave her. It concerned her resistance to changing the accent of her voice for a certain film she was about to make. The message made sense to her and she thanked me. One of the men with her was, I learned later, her husband – a young, hefty New Zealander called Bryan Southcombe. I did not imagine for a moment that he was to become a patient of mine for a symptom brought on by stress. This is one of the most unusual stories I can tell, for his problem was a curious one. I will relate the events as they occurred.

Some time after my meeting with Charlotte Rampling I was summoned to lunch at the beautifully-appointed villa which had been originally build as a French holiday home for her, Bryan and their son, Barnaby. Lying on a plateau amongst beautiful trees and a terraced garden which surrounded a welcoming swimming pool, the villa looked down and across a wide green valley which lies alongside the road running from St Tropez across the wide headland to the golden beaches of Pamplonne. As I heard that Bryan's marriage was having severe problems, I was not surprised to find no trace of Charlotte Rampling. I was instead led to the lunch table laid out by the pool by a mutual friend who had heard about my healing abilities and, I learned later, had invited me particularly to get to know Bryan. It was therefore quite natural that a short while later I should issue a small return invitation to my table.

I could see that Bryan was not at all fit. Much later when I grew to know Bryan better, he told me about the anguish of the divorce proceedings, involving as they did not only his former wife but also his son. On top of that, as a professional relations consultant he had to make long flights across the world with the ensuing jet-lag problems. To counter his lack of sleep he had consulted a doctor in Beverly Hills, California, who treated him with a mixture of valium and phenogen as a tranquillizer. The effect on Bryan, not used to strong medication was, to use his own words, 'a tranquillizer-induced state of torpor'.

'So now I had two problems,' he continued, 'the first was stress, the second was how to get off my tranquillizers. I knew I had to go cold turkey and cut out medication completely. I did not realize, however, the dramatic effect of this decision.'

So that evening at my dinner table I had before me a man who was not only a victim of stress due to his divorce, but added to that he was fighting withdrawal symptoms from a medication we now know to be addictive, valium. His predicament was growing worse each day. As he told me later, 'I did not know how long I could hold on. I had a brilliant white light burning in my skull. Although things were getting desperate I was determined not to get hooked on tranquillizers once more.'

The light, which he likened to 'a brilliant neon light' prevented Bryan from sleeping, for every time he closed his eyes it shone. He was trapped in this desperate situation between an ever-growing desire for the need of sleep, and the almost physical pain he suffered from the interior white light which switched on when he closed his eyes.

Bryan had at the time absolutely no faith at all in the powers of healing. The friend who had invited me to meet him had very tactfully not talked about the stories she had heard about my healing successes. Although the idea was to arrange for me to treat Bryan, he had come to dinner at my place as an excuse to make it easier for him to try just one treatment. At this point so dreadful did he feel, he had nothing to lose.

After the simple meal I cleared the table and sat Bryan in the folding director's chair I often use for guests. Raising my consciousness, I paused a moment before placing both my hands about his head. I remember being grateful as I felt the surge of power as the healing force manifested. Within a moment I saw Bryan relax as his shoulders dropped, his eyes closed. I will let him tell you in his own words what he experienced:

Imagine my amazement when, within a few seconds of Allon putting his hands on my head, I felt a curious heat emanating from them. Then just as if someone had clicked off a switch, the white light inside my head, the source of all my problems, went out. That night for the first time for months I went home and slept normally. All who have suffered from insomnia will know how dreadful is the fatigue, and how wonderful the relief when sleep returns.

Ever since that night now twelve years ago, I have been able to sleep normally. No-one can ever tell me now that healing doesn't work. Although I have heard since and read very much more about Allon Bacon's spiritual healing powers, what happened to me in those short moments are proof enough for me.

So many events in our lives, possibly the most significant, appear as if in accord with some hidden cosmic clock. Sometimes the clues are much less significant, and they often come in groups of three. Carl Jung calls it the law of synchronicity. An example of this brings this last healing story up-to-date.

Spending the late autumn in St Tropez preparing the last chapters of this book, I came across Bryan Southcombe all these years later whilst shopping in the vicinity. I accepted his invitation for a drink in the bar of the elegant Hotel Sube, one of the oldest hotels in the port, its facade in line with the central curve of the waterfront. Sitting in the lounge cum dining room near a log fire in the huge old fireplace, we gazed down at the magnificent view of the port with its many yachts anchored below for the winter. Above our heads in the bar maritime flags of all nations fluttered, reminding us that the bar is also the headquarters for a yacht club.

Bryan and I talked about the *Nioulargue*, the fairly recently created yacht race started by a local, Patrice de Colmont, who also helps run his family's discreet but chic beach restaurant, Club 55. Bryan was present at and encouraged the inauguration of this race which he helps to run, a race which now is attracting richly-backed and superb yachts from Britain, America, France and all over the world.

Knowing that Charlotte Rampling had long since married the French composer Jean-Michel Jarre and now lived in a large residence west of Paris, I was surprised and delighted to meet again her son Barnaby who suddenly walked into the bar to see his father Bryan. A little later his mother and step-father drove up along the quay-side below to take Barnaby back to the villa where I had originally met Bryan.

As I was talking to Bryan about stories for this book, he willingly agreed to sign a testimony of those events which marked his life twelve years ago and the healing at my hands which we both welcomed.

To complete the law of synchronicity, a few nights later (Monday of this week) French television showed Visconti's powerful film *The Damned* starring amongst others Charlotte Rampling. As I sat watching it I cast a glance at my director's chair folded in its resting place by my cluttered writing table, happy to see this page telling Bryan's healing story adding to the ever-growing pile of the manuscript of this book. As a writer I am eternally grateful that my life as a healer hands me, almost every day, new and fascinating material which I can sometimes share to try to awaken understanding and enlightenment in others, and hopefully entertainment as well.

Helping the Dying

As all healers will tell you, the main object of the healing work is to help people get better. Sometimes it is our task to help them die. In so many instances I have noticed that healing given to the very sick can be of great service in many ways. As a good minister, of whatever religion, can bring by his presence calm and courage to the dying, so can a healer. In my experience it is not always desirable to talk over much with them. Presence is the key word. You are willing by your presence to share with them some of the often deep emotions they are feeling. A friendly hand held in silence can work wonders. It goes without saying that the hand is offering and giving healing. On more than one occasion I have noticed that, for example, someone dying of cancer will not need that final pain-killing draught given in mercy by a caring doctor. To the surprise of the nurse and the doctor, the patient simply sleeps naturally into the change we call death. The healing power has done its wonderful work once again.

One could write at much greater length about this solemn and important moment we call, for lack of a better word, death. When I am sending or giving healing to the dying, I try also to concentrate on the creative side of the process. For a person dying here is preparing for their new birthday in another existence. People love to say that no-one has ever come back to tell us about death. For a medium this is totally untrue. Many people have communicated with me and told me what they can about the process. My Aunt Gwen, for example, with whom I shared so many early adventures into psychic enquiry left this world recently at a good old age. She communicated with me merely a few days after, telling that leaving her arthritic-bound legs was like stepping out of wet, heavy sand-bags; the feeling of relief and freedom after her years of brave struggling against disease was, she said, tremendous. So many people who have medically died and then been resuscitated have testified about floating towards a great white light which felt like the presence of total love before they were called back. So many people have testified to having floated away from their bodies attached by a silver cord, leaving them lying clearly visible on the operating-theatre bed. We are born attached to our mothers by the umbilical cord which after severance is discarded. We die when the spiritual cord attaching our newly-separated etheric body, invisible to the human eye, floats off to find its new existence on another time level. Both are a different kind of birth.

The reader of this book alone knows of the testimonies of Vivien Leigh and Frederick Lennon, when communicating to me emotions and thoughts about the process.

If I am in the presence of a dying person who would simply be confused by any talk about arriving in another world, I naturally would not burden them with those thoughts. Sometimes it is in a person's destiny to have to discover about the next world when they get to it. There are a vast group of trained workers on the other side whose work is to welcome the souls coming over and make them as comfortable as possible whilst they are resting and later being prepared for their new life with all its vast possibilities.

My Aunt Gwen likened her arrival to that of being greeted in a reception area halfway between an airport lounge and a hospital. Souls of all nationalities were coming in and being welcomed from all over planet Earth. She was taken by skilled workers to an area of privacy with a decor of her choice to rest before the excitement of rejoining her loved ones gone before.

Sometimes I talk to the dying about being met on the other side by their loved ones, if I sense they can accept this. A sweet little Irish lady dying of widespread cancer came to me last summer for treatment. After her last brave visit to my sanctuary, about the fifth, she asked me to visit her at home. This I did. Once I had explained she would not arrive in the next world alone, her face lit up with joy.

'Promise me? You're not just saying it?'

'Promise you. Just see,' I replied.

The little lady died about three weeks later. It was her loving sister-in-law, who was with her at the time, who finished this part of her story:

She was sinking into a sort of coma and then floating back up to see me. Then as she held my hand in deep sleep, she suddenly sat up in bed opening wide her eyes and her arms as if she'd seen someone I could not see. At that moment with a smile she called out, 'Hello' and as if trying to grasp at some invisible person ahead of her, she fell back and she was gone. It was the most beautiful thing I have experienced in my life.

My advice to healers being asked to help patients die is very simple. Share time with them, sometimes in silence. Hold their hand or not as the occasion and the mood presents. Answer their questions as best you can, but remember it is rarely wise to lie to them. Better to remain quiet. Overall give them the healing their soul needs to live through the change it is having to face as the failing vehicle of their body finally breaks down and comes to a halt, thus liberating them for their new birthday. I always wish the departing 'Bon Voyage' and I know I am privileged when as a medium I receive their thanks on their safe arrival.

Rescue Service

Another part of the work which sometimes befalls a healer or a medium is what we term 'rescue service'. As there are companies who send out trained men to rescue stranded motorists, psychics are sometimes used to rescue stranded souls. There are occasions when for one reason or another, due to shock, ignorance or the need of the experience for soul development, a soul has to be rescued from, shall we say, 'the corridors of time'. One of the purposes of spiritual instruction is to help people die. When this has not been accomplished, some people need rescuing.

Rescue service is a great drain on psychic energy and must only be undertaken in limited amounts. Some people recommend it should only be undertaken in the presence of other mediums and/or healers. Any trainee healer or medium reading this section who feels drawn to this work must seek advice from their teacher who should be thoroughly versed in such matters to be of proper use as a counsellor. If there is any doubt then all concerned should leave this part of psychic work particularly well alone. It is work only for the strong and the properly guided.

My first solo rescue took place many years ago whilst I was in France having finished my training in my healing circle. During meditation there came to me a communication in sight and sound from a young French officer in the army, who had been captured and tortured during the war in French Malaya known as the 'forgotten war'. Because of my state of raised consciousness the fellow saw my light signal (an easy way of describing it) and came literally stumbling towards me, completely lost. He was in fact what we call dead, but he had not yet for one reason or the other, grasped the fact. The spiritual body which met me was a horrendous sight of despair and suffering, as he had still about him every detail of his wounded, uniformed presence resembling the body in which he had died. The world might refer to him therefore as a ghost. It would take too long to give all the details of the story he poured out to me as he collapsed, crying out in total despair. In brief, he had been separated from his unit in the jungle fighting and hidden by a native girl who finally had let him go. On his way through the jungle to try to regain his unit, he came across a dead soldier from whose body he stole a watch. Captured again by the enemy, he was tortured in a terrible manner which involved taking the prayer book he carried in his tropical kit top-pocket and desecrating it inside a huge chest wound inflicted by his barbaric capturers. As he lay dying his religious convictions were giving him terrible guilt from having had sex with the girl who hid him, and having stolen the watch from his dead fellow soldier. So he died in agony, considering himself in a state of sin, and because of the stressful manner and circumstance of his passing, he could not ascertain whether he was dead or in a transient state of suffering somewhere between two time levels.

I explained to the soldier that he was indeed dead, and that he must now be helped to move towards his new life in spirit. Spiritual help was brought to him as he was able to accept his passing and prepare for a whole new life, having cast off his condition.

Months later, during meditation, the soldier contacted me in spirit form showing himself calm, healed, and wanting to thank me for his rescue. I explained I was just one of a team, and that too a part of the brotherhood of workers in this field. He is now himself working in the rescue service on the next time level, helping fellow soldiers across from a sudden death into their new existence. This one story gives you an idea of rescue service, and why it can only be undertaken in limited amounts.

House clearing and site clearing

If you think I mean by this phrase that I am going to write about the clearing of unwanted furniture and rubbish left behind by the previous occupiers of a dwelling, that is not the case! Except that, on another level, there is a resemblance. I mean, of course, to talk about clearing a residence or site of unwanted vibrations, using my psychic energies for a different kind of healing to that of de-haunting.

I believe there are two main categories of cases involving haunting. The first involves the replay of time memories registered in the walls of an old building or previous events which might have taken place on that site. A sensitive can be troubled by these replays. People who are psychically aware of previous dramas in a place can often see what are commonly known as ghosts, for this reason.

The second category of haunting can be manifestations caused by troubled spirits who for one reason or another have a fixation about returning to a certain place where they might have experienced some great emotion. Thus they are held back from getting on with their new lives on the next plane. They are fixated by the past.

In either case I invoke the white light of cosmic energy to shine about the place or the spirit of the haunting presence. In my experience, freeing an obsessed spirit and helping them overcome their obsession to move on to a fuller life is easier than erasing time memories from a site.

There is a country road in Sussex near to where I live which throws up such strong visions about me as I travel there, that I now have learned to switch them off to avoid them impinging on my sensitivity. The play-backs are those of a fierce battle which ranges from this particular part of the downs country and to a town called Lewes. The soldiers involved are carrying huge cross-swords and metal shields and wearing metal and leather helmets with strips of protective metal over their noses. Chain-mail shirts and every kind of armour from full suits to chest and shoulder and leg protectors are worn. The noise of the battle is enormous. Horses bearing armoured men wielding their huge swords rear up about me as I receive the full blast of the time replay. It is hideous to see terrible wounds being inflicted on the men as they fall off their steeds, or as some fight or fall on foot. The cries from the wounded horses disturb me greatly as the battle rages about me whilst driving or walking past the site. So intense is the play-back that I have wondered if I myself was not involved in that particular battle on a past time level. I am giving some of the lurid details of this time experience to explain the intense emotion involved in the replay. I would not think I could ever erase those vibrations from that site, so deeply are they recorded. But I have resolved the problem of my involvement and I can now protect myself from the horror of passing that site. I notice with concern that the site attracts very risky driving from motorists using the road who may be unwittingly affected by the strong psychic vibrations emanating from the soil there. Having witnessed some reckless behaviour from nearby motorists I now send out regular prayers for protection to all those using that road.

Sometimes I am invited to de-haunt some specific site. The first time involved a haunting which was preventing hefty building workers from being willing to continue with the alterations being carried out in a huge, elegant, period house in a sea-side town further down the coast from where I live. The workers were being disturbed by two women's voices who kept crying out in the building. I picked up a story of an illegitimate girl who was kept locked away in one wing of the house in times past. A house-keeper companion was given the task of caring for the girl, who was occasionally produced in front of house-guests as a live-in maid, a fact she deeply resented. My knees felt quite weak as I trod the stairs leading to a top room beside one tower-like part of the building, and also in a period grotto with a metal grille front adjoining the large grounds which surrounded the house. I worked psychically for the release of these troubled spirits, and I won. The voices disappeared, the feeling in the house became warm and homely, and the workers resumed work. A year later I was to spend the night in a newly-created room occupying a part of the haunted tower, and I slept deeply and peacefully. The owner was grateful with the new feeling of peace in his newly-acquired property. I believe some sheets of music were occasionally moved on the grand piano in the ball-room. But nobody minds that after what had taken place. And after all it might have been the wind wafting in on a summer's evening from the huge and wide windows. Imagination and fact touch fingers lightly in these cases, which is, I suppose, why these stories hold such fascination for so many people, and why they always will.

I would not now choose to be involved in too many similar events. The experience in the above case, and in several more I could relate, has been useful for me as a psychic trying to solve the mysteries of etheric energy, time levels and personal spiritual problems of evolvement. But on the whole I feel my healing powers should be used on people who need help in terms of illness, rather than de-haunting houses. There is enough human suffering here and now to be dealt with, without getting fixated on events over and done with these many years. I am, of course, happy to have had the chance to help some suffering spirit forms. Except for rare cases, however, I prefer to work on the now rather than on the then – perhaps expressed better by saying I would rather help people and animals than be a house and site clearer.

Animal Healing

The relationship between man and animal has always been very complex. On planet Earth we sometimes love them as pets, use them for a way of living, hunt them cruelly to death, vivisect them, use them for scientific tests, or simply kill them to eat.

As this century draws to an end, bringing with it so many radical changes concerning man and his relationship with and responsibility to his environment, many people are being alerted to our hypocritical and two-channelled approach to the animal kingdom. On the one hand we need them and sometimes love them, on the other we use them solely to suit our ends. As we evolve, there is no doubt in my mind that our relationship with the animal kingdom must and will change. Vast numbers of people have already given up eating meat (though some will merrily eat fish killed for that purpose) and a growing consciousness regarding our exterminating, or almost, many wonderful species is happily manifesting. It is a very complex situation involving commercial interest, personal conscience and habit, and growing awareness of our two-track behaviour. A swiftly-growing number of people across the world are already acting on their conscience and working with all their energy raising resources to help put right the situation. Vast prayer energy is also being used on more than one time level to alert man to treat the animal kingdom more correctly. It was revealing just recently to see that the fate of three trapped whales brought the costly resources of two great nations, the USA and USSR to work together. 'Save the whale' is a known slogan – could it be that the animal kingdom, ranging from the most primitive to the more intelligently evolved, has its instinctive slogan, 'Save man'? For in treating animals badly we are building up for ourselves a vast karma which has to be paid on one time level or another.

As I am writing this in St Tropez I am constantly reminded that one of my neighbours a few kilometres away is now concentrating a lot of her time and energy to work for the animals. Her name, Brigitte Bardot.

Bardot is one of the most famous women in the world; as a symbol for France she rivals the Eiffel Tower for Paris. Even now it is difficult for her to appear in public, certainly during the season here, without a crowd of camera-snapping tourists appearing from nowhere.* Like many other full- or part-time locals I have exchanged the odd word with her whilst happening alongside her choosing something in the market, something she likes to do out of season. I have special memories of her tying up her boat and steping off, bikini clad, onto the quay a few metres away from my balcony. Once I glimpsed her sun-bathing with a

---

*Bardot has since announced she will sell up her St Tropez property owing to lack of privacy.

group of friends whom she had encouraged to swim on the beach beside her small property, *La Madrague*. Stretched out in the sun with her golden hair falling about her, she resembled a fine Renoir. Even driving her jeep-like vehicle filled with English setters, her back held straight like the trained dancer she is, she holds the attention. The flapping dogs' ears, mixing with her flowing locks, made a fitting frame to her famous features. If cynical tongues say she has taken to animals having failed with some of her human relationships, I would reply that her demonstrated love for them does not set a bad example for a retired but still living legend.

An animal can choose to give its affection or not to a human being. It is not impressed by fame. There is no conflict either with an animal concerning religious or sectarian hang-ups. The animal kingdom has its own instinctive and guileless approach to the great mysteries of life. An animal patient for healing is as trusting and innocent as a child. With their minds un-cluttered with bigotry they are a joy to treat either with the laying on of hands or by absent healing. They sense immediately the vibrations carried and emanating from a healer, and respond accordingly. Everywhere I go they greet me. They know and demonstrate their instinctive trust. What is more animals give out healing to each other, and, when they choose, to the human race.

Apart from an animal giving its healing presence to its present owner, they often attend, in spirit form, a healing session with their former master or mistress. They come in spirit form to witness me healing their human friend as well as to contribute with their loving presence. When I choose to describe their presence to my human patient, the person is invariably happy to know that the link between them and their assumed dead animal friend continues.

Animals too have been known, whilst here in the flesh, to demonstrate individual characteristics of another animal previously owned by their master. They have a highly-developed sixth sense, as well as sometimes acting as mediums and healers themselves.

I remember one woman in particular who came to me for healing. She must have been in her seventies, and her visit caused my healing sanctuary to be filled with the spirit forms of horses who stood with their heads together forming a circle about me and my patient. At the last moment a dappled grey horse arrived in spirit form, the other horses making way for him to stand with his head just beside and above my patient. Being so impressed by the experience I told my patient what I could see with my third eye.

'I'm not in the least surprised,' the woman said calmly with a smile. 'The breeding and training of horses has been my entire life. And that dappled grey was my favourite.'

Because of the migrant pattern of my life, I cannot have a dog. The quarantine laws for re-entry into Britain necessitate a six-month stay in quarantine for domestic animals, a precaution against rabies. Until a few years ago one was, however, allowed to travel with a caged bird. An extraordinary budgerigar who flew by chance into my open kitchen window in Brighton many years ago became my companion for twelve years. He spoke phrases in English and French, and became as close to being human as he could, tasting my food and my drink. He used to roar with laughter at certain television news-readers and imitated me speaking on the telephone. My healing hands brought him through two serious attacks, but when eventually he died in my presence I gave him a funeral at sea. His spirit form has shown itself to me more than once, as well as occasionally manifesting through the mediumship of a later bird I adopted to try to fill the gap of his loss. Tweetie-Pie, as I christened him, was an incredible companion who was, I know, sent to me to share some lonely and difficult years, which he did superbly well. I owe him a great debt of gratitude and wish him well as his little soul evolves through the time levels and the destiny awaiting him.

As so many people, particularly the elderly and the lonely, wonder if they will be rejoined with their pets in the hereafter my answer to them is an undoubted yes. Animals have their full place in the next world, and the bond of love which links us to them cannot be severed by time. We can rejoin our loved animals as we can our loved friends and relatives. We all evolve together. They know full well about our prayers for them and they link with us in their thoughts and memories.

I would like here to include some animal healing stories which I think will interest all animal lovers.

By chance, or rather by synchronicity, I am tomorrow lunching with the owners of a little brown dog called Tamara, with the purpose of listening to the broadcast I put on tape recently in Monte Carlo for Radio Riviera. Hearing the advance trailer of the programme, the Odells kindly rang me with the friendly idea of us all listening together. As any broadcaster will tell you, listening to yourself can be nerve-racking, and as this is the first broadcast I have recorded in English in France or in Monaco, I accepted with pleasure. Although I did not talk about Tamara particularly, it was because of this little dog I came to know her owners.

Tamara

I remember my first meeting with Tamara, a little coffee-coloured dog who has a lot of spaniel in her appearance, seven years ago. I had been talking to John Odell on the telephone concerning word processors as he is an expert in such things. During the course of the conversation he kindly invited me to tea. Such an invitation for an Englishman is always welcome in France. In the same way that the English are only just learning to offer a decent cup of coffee worth its name, so the French are not always expert at making tea. They like to pour hot water onto the tea instead of warming the pot first, and then adding boiling water. So, the next day at four o'clock I was received by the English couple, the Odells, in their charming home tucked away in forestland at the bottom of the long hill road which climbs steeply up to Gassin, a hill village loved by the English, just a few kilometres behind St Tropez. As I sat in the cosy kitchen cum lounge, Anni Odell handed me my cup of tea which was very welcome, it being an autumn day.

Because my hosts had heard about my healing talents they pointed out the little brown dog seemingly asleep by the fireplace the other end of the room.

'Poor Tam, she's seized up with arthritis in her legs and in her back.'

I glanced across at the animal as John added, 'Tried everything, the poor beast has really gone downhill.' He said it as if he had accepted the change in the dog to be permanent.

Anni then told me how little Tam had completely lost her *joie-de-vivre*. 'I suppose you couldn't do anything for her?'

She looked down at the dog, and then at me with such anxiety that I was moved to reply, 'Wait and see if the dog gets up and comes to speak to me. That might give you your answer.'

It was quite five minutes later, after we had been talking about this and that, when Tamara got painfully up to waddle across the room towards me. Then with a deep sigh she stood in front of me and placed her head firmly onto my lap. Brown eyes were asking me for help.

'She never does that to anyone outside the family,' Anni said with surprise in her voice.

'I'm used to that,' I replied, 'I only have to walk into a strange house and all the animals make towards me.' I marvelled as I often do at the loving simplicity of so many animals. When they come to me for healing, their minds are not cluttered up with anxiety about religious denominations, or having to believe in this creed or that. As with children, they have beautifully direct and straightforward minds. If only more of us humans were as straightforward.

With Tam's stiff back now held before me I started to gently caress the dog. She stood with her head on my lap as if she knew exactly what I was doing, and why she had approached me. We enjoyed the moment of communion, as I have enjoyed so very many such times when a sick animal puts its trust in you. I asked that my healing hands help this little dog, obviously such a loved member of the Odell family.

I suppose four or five minutes had passed when Tamara gently lifted up her head, turned around and waddled back to her previous place by the fire. Then with a satisfied grunt she once more stretched out on the rug. Letting out a deep sigh of relief, she immediately went to sleep.

As I travelled back to Britain very shortly after the events described above, I heard nothing about Tam for a while. Then from a mutual friend I heard the dog had from the following day made a wonderful recovery. She was leaping about again looking and behaving like a dog years younger. Tamara had found again her love of life. I was delighted, and even more pleased to receive a charming letter of thanks a little later.

The Odells have since built themselves a lovely home set on the edge of vineyards and trees not far from their old residence. Tamara is still living happily with them. If the passing years have brought the odd twinge and certain days of less activity, she is still very much enjoying her life, particularly as she has a charming black labrador now to play with.

My visit with them yesterday to listen to the broadcast went well. Tam, who ran out to greet me, immediately went back to the living room to roll on her back smiling as we sat round the pine table for a chat before our meal. I noticed that she seemed unmoved by my voice coming over the air from Monte Carlo. After all she didn't have to be told, she knows I am a healer. And I know that for seven years I have had another four-footed friend.

NOBBY THE CAT

Nobby the cat provided me with one of the most extraordinary series of animal healing stories I have experienced. Series is the word I chose specially. The special circumstances of this particular story are to me made all the more touching by the fact that Nobby became a personality in my life, although for years I had not met him. He was simply another animal on my absent healing list. But by the very nature of the events that followed, it is inaccurate to say even that, for Nobby became more of a living legend.

Those of you who have followed my healing story will remember that I met and gave healing to a certain Clive Hill, a event which turned out to be of great importance to me in the acceptance of my healing gift. It so happened that Clive possessed a much loved cat, already middle-aged, who became ill after Clive's own healing. It was therefore natural for him to contact me. As circumstances of distance and travel for a cat were complicated, I put Nobby on my healing list. His name came up amongst the others for whom and to whom I sent out my healing energies. Each time Nobby became ill, this routine was followed. And each time Nobby made a recovery. Through the years, the matter became almost routine, except that I consider no healing in that manner. I am hopefully full of gratitude and joy each time anyone receives benefit from my healing powers, however often this might occur. So it was that Nobby the black cat suffered from stomach problems, kidney problems, more than one stroke. The vet was often consulted and gave his treatment too. But it must be said that during the eight years about which I am writing, Nobby was often as good as given up. Each time the vet warned Clive the case was fairly hopeless, each time he contacted me for absent healing, and each time the cat made extraordinary progress back to good health. A Saturday night might see him stretched out in a state of collapse after perhaps a haemorrhage or a heart attack, but by the following Tuesday, shall we say, he was once more prowling about the garden taking an interest in life and eating normally. After a whole series of such events, the vet finally hesitated to say anything, so used was he to the cat's extraordinary powers of recovery. So Nobby became a living legend amongst us all. He hated travel, and as Clive had to move more than once during these three years, he was nervous of upsetting the cat. Each time a journey was anticipated Clive contacted me for help, and each time Nobby climbed into and out of his travelling basket as if he had suffered nothing unusual to disturb his equilibrium.

So it was that one Christmas a few years ago I was invited to lunch in the country cottage where Clive and his mother were living, to meet Nobby. I will always remember my first sight of the cat in flesh and blood, as they say. For I had previously glimpsed him from a distance with my third eye, a circumstance which sometimes happens when I am meditating. As I entered the kitchen-dining room Nobby was sitting on a cushion placed on the draining-board by the sink. There was this splendid animal staring at me in the face with his huge eyes. As if he were expecting me he signalled my arrival with one huge meouw. The sound he made was the nearest thing to a human hello that I have ever heard from the throat of a cat. From the time I sat down to eat to the moment I left later that day, Nobby seemed to be enjoying staring at me. It was as if he understood completely that the luncheon was being given for us to meet, and for him to have the chance to thank me personally for what I had been allowed to do for him.

Nobby became ill again not so very long after our meeting. This time I sensed it was terminal. He died peacefully shortly afterwards and was duly buried, I am told, with love and respect under a favourite tree. You can see now why he became so special. As with so many of my patients, I think of him from time to time and wonder what sort of after-life is his now. I am sure too he sometimes thinks of us here. He had, after all, spent eighteen years on planet Earth, and that, even for a cat like Nobby, is a long time.

The Blind Dog

My next animal healing story I tell in all its simplicity, realizing only too well that that is the only way it can be told. Even then I almost hesitate to put the facts down again on paper. It is as if they are in a way too marvellous to contemplate. A healer must be often torn between a sense of wonder and gratitude and a desire to share good news. I would not wish in telling this next story to raise false hopes in the minds of others. And yet I must always be deeply touched that it happened. Here are the facts as I know them.

I was in France working on a manuscript when I received a letter from a lady in Scotland asking me to put the name of her dog on my absent healing list. She told me in her letter that the dog had recently become blind. I remember thinking as I sent out prayers to the dog, what really am I expected to do for a blind dog sitting here at my writing desk so far away from Scotland? It was perhaps a moment of human weakness, perhaps also a moment of challenge. I remember immediately correcting my thought and changing it into a postive one. I remember thinking also of Jesus the great healer who more than once caused the blind to see and wishing I could be allowed to use my healing powers to help this much loved pet stumbling about his home. Then I thought, why not? Jesus after all told us, 'Do as I do.' I tried to picture the simplicity and faith of this great healer ready to face any challenge. Then having put my healing thoughts into action and sent off my message of corrective energy towards the dog, I went back to work on my book.

It was two or three months later that I received the letter telling me that the dog had completely recovered her sight.

'She is back to her usual happy self,' the owner wrote in thanking me, 'full of fun and eager to get out in the country and sniff out rabbits. We still look at her and can hardly believe she was totally blind for about three months.'

You can understand now my hesitancy to tell the story. You may understand also the desire to share it with you. It was to me one of the greatest lessons that we must never ever limit the possibility of the power of prayer energy and prayer action. It would not be right for us to do so.

11.
HOW TO MEDITATE AND SOME SUGGESTED MEDITATIONS

SEVERAL times in this book I have talked about meditating. There may be some readers who are new to the word or to the act of meditation. These following pages give me a chance to explain what meditation consists of, how to learn to meditate, and some suggested guidelines for various meditations.

Meditation is a technique of raising the vibrations of your consciousness to give out or to receive the energy some refer to as prayer. It can also be described as a heightened consciousness of being. The process of meditation as a project fills many people with awe. It is in fact one of the simplest of states to achieve, and one of the most worthwhile. It is an excellent technique for advancing your spiritual awareness, and your power to heal yourself or to help others. Some people, for various reasons, have tried to make it sound difficult. It need not be. Riding a bicycle seems difficult to those who cannot. To those who can, it seems simple. Meditation can be compared to that.

Once you become conscious of it, breathing can be an effort. Otherwise, for those in good health, breathing is effortless. Meditating is similiar. Once you have learned to shift your consciousness into the gear of meditation you can stay there with practice for as long or as short a time as you need or want.

One of the secrets of practice is regularity. Choose the same time each day for trying it and stick to it. Once the pattern of regular meditation is achieved, then you may allow yourself flexibility. Similarly, for the beginner, trying to meditate in the same place each time is helpful. After you achieve results you can meditate in widely different circumstances. Let me offer you some further hints to help you master meditation.

If you choose to be at home, try for a quiet corner where if possible you are alone (unless you are with your meditating partner or group). Choose if possible a straight-backed, not too comfortable chair. Meditation must not be confused with relaxation. Do not save meditation for bed-time, you will confuse your self-programming and may end up asleep. Excellent though sleep is, it is not the purpose of meditation.

Wear clothes which are preferably loose and comfortable. If male, loosen your tie, should you happen to be wearing one. Ladies should similarly make themselves comfortable particularly about the neck, waist and feet. All should kick off their shoes and remove tailored jackets. Be at ease.

I personally like to meditate to music, my choice being anything harmonious and played softly. Rock and roll would not be my choice – leave that for dancing!

If you can, take the telephone off the hook. Do not have a bright light shining on your face. Dimming the lights, if indoors at night, can be very helpful. Burning sweet-smelling incense helps many people to meditate, but, like many physical aids, it is not in any way essential.

Having placed yourself in your sitting position, order your body to relax. Achieve this in stages. I teach people to start with their feet. If it helps, whisper aloud the command, 'Relax feet.' Now, 'Relax ankles.' Move slowly up the body obeying the commands as they progress. When you arrive at 'Relax chin, relax neck, relax face', you may find your head wants to fall gently back or gently forward. Providing your breathing is in no way impaired, let this happen. If your breathing feels impaired, then adjust your head to its normal position and keep it balanced there effortlessly.

With the command, 'Relax eyes', close them gently. Be sure you have travelled down the arms and relaxed shoulders, elbows, wrists and hands. Some people let their hands and arms swing loose, vertical with the floor. Others prefer to have their wrists and hands laying gently on their laps. Do what comes naturally in this respect.

Once the whole body is beautifully relaxed, slow and deepen your breathing. Be conscious of trying to fill all of your lungs, particularly the lower part. (See note on Diaphragm Breathing.) It is preferable to breathe in through your nose and not through your mouth. Stay relaxed and breathing deeply and slowly. Do not exaggerate your breathing to the point of feeling dizzy.

Should this happen, stop the deep breathing immediately, breathe normally for a while, move about gently in your chair, then relax and start again breathing less deeply this time. This process of relaxing the body and going into deep breathing will have taken no longer than one minute as I teach it.

The next command is 'Relax mind'. As this command is sometimes the most difficult for beginners to achieve, I can give you some techniques to help you. The best way to relax your mind, is to empty it. At first this will be near impossible. Ideas will float in like unwanted waste paper in the breeze. Therefore instead of trying to empty the mind as such, empty it by filling it with a picture. Imagine something of beauty and of peace. I do not advise imagining the beauty of a human form, as this can lead to other thoughts not required in this exercise. A good symbol to gaze at in your mind is a flower. I teach a rose, because it is the symbol of spiritual love and it is more or less internationally known. Some may prefer to choose a red or a white rose, others one of the pastel shades. Place the rose if you like in your imagination in a glass of water. Smell its perfume in your mind, regard the beauty of its texture, see possibly a drop of moisture on a leaf growing from its stem. Enjoy it. After achieving this, try to move round it in your mind. When the exercise becomes easier, float up in your mind a little above the rose and gaze down upon it. Do not let yourself float up and away. Should this start to happen bring yourself immediately but gently back. Remember in this exercise I am teaching you meditation and nothing further.

Some people prefer to picture a scene of peace and beauty instead of a flower. A lake lying below a mountain can be a very good scene for some. I have often known people choose a particular lake they once visited on a holiday. This can be a good aid to meditation, but remember I am not asking you at this time to re-live a particular holiday. I am teaching you to meditate.

The golden rule is to commence meditating a little at a time. Start with two minutes, extend to three. After a week move on to five minutes. Some people find it easy to meditate for twenty minutes, others find it hard to try for three. Everyone must find their level. Five or ten minutes of good meditation is better than twenty minutes of third-rate meditation. The purpose of the exercise is to raise your consciousness so that you are in an altered state. In this altered state you are living in a way which encourages you to vibrate well with your spiritual or etheric body. Once this happens you are achieving a moment of extended consciousness. Enjoy it.

The experiences and 'work' you can achieve once the state of raised consciousness has been reached through meditation are endless. Should you be a person with an already-adopted discipline of religion with its prayer formula, prayers offered in this altered state are well launched. The great mysteries can be thought about, the reflection of the Divine Mind can be held and sustained. Thus each individual faith can be expressed. Meditation can be used for just this purpose.

Some people choose to use meditation simply for relaxation without trying to understand its deeper purpose. There is nothing wrong with this. One day they may be inspired quite suddenly to extend their relationship with their God. If they have not envisaged a God, they may seek to find one. So one and all can link up with the Cosmic Energy about us available for the asking.

Everyday energy can be given a boost through meditation and inspiration for work can be increased. The task of harmonizing relationships of every kind can be worked upon. Ideas can be brought up from the subconscious at a later date, having been ordered to surface during meditation. Programming of every kind can be beneficially undertaken. Sportsmen can encourage their stamina, businessmen their acumen, housewives their talents in running a good home for their loved ones. The variety and purpose to which meditation can be put is as endless as time. But, being a healer, I encourage meditation to be used for the cultivation and care of good positive health for people of all ages.

The value of meditation is beyond expression. Try it. Start today.

NOTE ON DIAPHRAGM BREATHING

This technique of filling the bottom of the lungs with air to achieve an overall greater lung capacity, can be studied separately. Meditation does not depend on it, but its mastery and use can help. It is also a useful technique for singers, actors and athletes of all kinds, as well as for helping asthmatics, bronchial patients, etc. As a healer I respect its value for increasing the life force. I have used it as a tool for self-healing, public-speaking, singing and sport as well as for meditation.

In mastering the technique of diaphragm breathing, one learns to push out the stomach gently at the same time as one breathes in. A slow gentle rhythm is helpful, and gently does it. It helps to picture the diaphragm being, as it is, an elastic wall of tissue dividing the bottom of the lung cavity from the stomach. Pushing out the stomach as you breath in allows the diaphragm to stretch down, thus increasing the lung capacity at the base. To practise it, place your hand on your stomach as you exhale. The Eastern religions talk about taking in the *prana* or life force as you breathe in.

Having thus studied the technique of deep breathing, allied to the technique of relaxing and filling the mind with calm, I now suggest certain meditation outlines. I have placed one on each page to assist you to work on your meditating along these suggested lines of thought. They are only suggestions which might also lead you to invent meditations for yourself or, if you are meditating with a partner or in a group, also for colleagues. As you will see in the first suggested meditation, I accompany you, so that as your teacher we may get to know each other.

Meditation

LOAD SHARING AND DUMPING

This meditation came into my mind one day before I was to help someone who was going through great torment holding on to too many painful memories of the past. He told me he found it hard to meditate alone. So I felt inspired to teach him to share his meditations with me. This is how it goes.

Take a huge sack and place into it, one by one, all your regrets, griefs, wrong decisions, hurts from others, etc. I will help you load them all in.

So now we are standing together by a bridge. In my mind I use the Pont d'Iena in Paris, but any bridge will do. I now help you carry the sack to the centre of the bridge for it is too heavy for you alone. Together we lift it up and balance it on the parapet of the bridge, as we gaze below at the swiftly running water coming from over our shoulders away from us. You can now give the sack a push and watch it drop below splashing down into the river. Hang on to the parapet, don't go with the sack! Now watch the sack as it floats away, sinking as it does so. Eventually it disappears out of sight. Side by side we slowly walk back off the bridge where I leave you to resume your life.

The next time you do this meditation the sack should not need to be so large or heavy, and you should be able to carry it yourself and alone. I will wait at the end of the bridge to guide and encourage you. The third time you do the meditation (two days after the first – or whenever you choose) I want you to go completely alone. Yet we are never alone, so think of your guardian angel way up unseen in the sky watching over you.

Anti-Stress

A lot has been spoken and written recently about the damage done to health through stress. The average man has been made aware that stress raises the blood-pressure, causes heart attacks, erodes energy, etc. Too true. Stress can be blamed for a whole area of illness, both mental and physical, which attacks mankind. Stress is one of the prices man has to pay for living in the modern world. A jet can whisk a person from London to New York in so short a time that it takes his system much longer to recover. More stress. We drive our cars about roads so full of everyone doing the same that at times we want to shout at them. Stress.

We all have to learn to live with the possibility of stress trying to erode our calm and our energy and our health. The answer is, deal with it.

Meditation is one of the greatest weapons to fight stress. As we go into the relaxed state during meditation we are helping ourselves to eradicate stress. As a healer I can give you an anti-stress healing pill now. Go into meditation and imagine the pill is being made in front of you. Now take the imaginary pill and follow it with an imaginary glass of water. Delicious. Feel the pill relaxing you totally. Enjoy the sensation of the pill relaxing every part of your mind and your body. Float. Now enjoy the moment as your body is allowed to do its self-healing. Encourage every vital organ to work properly. Encourage the blood to be cleansed and to flow about your whole system. Ask it to adjust to its correct pressure. Feel your whole system enjoying the harmony of well-being. After a while come back to reality. You have done yourself a service.

Spiritual Pills

The technique I have just taught you to concentrate your self-healing energies on fighting stress can be extended to cover any disease. No mental exercise aimed at switching the body's working to positive is ever wasted. Even if it our destiny to be operated on for urgent surgery tomorrow, a self-healing exercise can help prepare ourselves and our bodies for just such an event. Even as we come out of the anaesthetic we can help ourselves to heal quickly and well.

By sitting calmly in meditation – or, if the circumstances dictate, by lying calmly – the technique of giving yourself a spiritual pill especially made for you now can be of utmost benefit to prepare you for any eventuality. If you respond to this idea, why not imagine my hands mixing the formula and making this pill for you. Picture me putting the spiritual ingredients needed into a bowl. Watch as I pound and mix them for you personally. With scrubbed clean hands I spoon out a portion to roll you a small pill. Watch my hands as I make your spiritual pill. In your mind, take it from me, swallow it, and now take the cool glass of water. Imagine the spiritual medicine activating your body to produce the substances needed to heal your disease. Hold this picture for five minutes. Relax. End of meditation.

Mind Weeding

Being a great gardener, I know I have to constantly weed my flower and vegetable beds to allow what I am encouraging to grow and to flourish. Take a tip from this gardener and weed your mind. Start now. Do not let negative thoughts get a stranglehold on you. Weed them out.

You think you are starting a cold. That is a weed, pull it out. You are frightened of developing this disease or that, that is a weed thought, pull it out. You are feeling down and you imagine yourself overcome by loneliness. That is a weed, pull it out.

Keep the bed of your mind free of these weed thoughts. Attend to this every day. Soon it becomes a way of life.

What you are achieving is programming your own mind and body to flourish. Work at it. Weeding works wonders. Try it. Start today. Start now. Get weeding.

(The above meditation is dedicated with thanks to Anni Odell, whose favourite it is.)

VARIETY

Boredom is a killer. Holidays are essential to take us away from the daily grind. If you cannot afford a holiday, try to change the routine even for a day. The wise masters of the past told us to rest on Sundays. In the pressure of modern life a lot of us have to work every day. Try to get some part of the routine altered. If you have time for your favourite walk, try an alteration in the route. Switch from your usual programme on your radio, try another.

Variety can be encouraged in so many ways. Try planting some seeds in a pot on your window ledge you have not attempted before. Try cooking a new dish. Listen to different music. You might not like it so much, but you will go back to your accustomed choice refreshed. Go to the library and read some new subject.

Meditate on variety and you will be inspired to invent all sorts of simple ways to achieve it. In so doing your attitude to yourself, your life and your partner or friends will be refreshed. So will your vital energies and thus your health.

Live Now

One of the commands I have tried to feed into my personal computer consists of two words: live now.

We are allowed to look back and learn from the past, but that is all. Happy memories are good, but regrets are useless. For your health's sake, give up chewing over the past, it may have gone stale. The fresh moments of today are much better for you.

Live now. The future holds hope. If the future also holds anxieties, worry about those when you get to them. Those famous words, 'Sufficient unto the day is the evil thereof', are charged with wisdom. Use this wisdom. Live now.

THINK UP

The great leaders of the world, the great star entertainers, all these have the quality of being able to think UP. Star quality is of course a special gift of providence, so is great leadership. But whatever our station in life, the habit of thinking UP can be cultivated within us all. Sit quietly, and think about the best you can offer to your world, whatever it be. Practice now in the quietness. Think UP. Offer to the world your best, your highest thoughts, the best of your brain power, your strongest prayers for the best of the forces about you. Think UP. Make it a regular part of your daily discipline. Soon you will find those thoughts are leading you to live UP. Offer your best, and the world will offer you its best. Avoid the second best. Think UP. Now, learn with your inner drives to stay UP.

When a great entertainer walks upon a platform, the stage, or in front of the camera, a change takes place within them. They shift from their ordinary drive to overdrive. They demonstrate their capacity to illuminate their aura so that it shines about them. To project their personalities they have learned to raise their vibrations and give out their particular radiance. They think UP and give OUT.

I remember once standing quietly at some occasion where I was by chance close to a singer with a world-famous name. She happened to be pregnant, and whereas that condition produces a radiance in some women, with her it did not. She was looking not at all her best. As there happened to be a group of musicians in the gathering who had spotted her presence, unbidden by her they started to play one of the songs she had made well-known. Then a strange thing happened. I can see her face changing in my memory as I write this. The star in question took in a deep breath, suddenly overcame the problems her pregnancy seemed to hold for her, and she took on before my eyes a look of radiance. Projecting her personality to the gathering, she created the song. After receiving her applause at the close she then seemed to step down back into her problems. Meanwhile she had given us more than a glimpse of her very best. She had thought UP and given OUT. It was an extraordinary demonstration of star quality. Her name – Shirley Bassey.

Think Well, Think Young

These two commands are useful ones to feed into your spiritual computer. Self-healing can be thought of as a good preventative for escaping the assault of illness, and of ageing. Having accustomed yourself to meditation, a useful time can be given to just these two programmes.

People accept the law of ageing as if it were something to be hurriedly got on with like a meal. Of course the stages of life, from birth to maturity and finally to death of the body, are inevitable. But it need not be inevitable that at middle age one has a fat stomach and that old age brings deafness, lack of energy and depression, to say the least. Old age can also bring serenity, wisdom, joy of helping others along the path, time to read and garden and learn new subjects.

Meditate on this positive programme. Start now. Whatever your age, eighteen or ninety, you are doing yourself a service. Think young, stay young. Hold this idea in your mind during meditation and you will be improving your programme. Then think well and stay well.

ENERGY

Hold in your mind the fact that nothing is achieved without energy. Energy is the driving force of the Cosmos without us and within us. Right to the last planet and star in our vision and beyond, energy abounds. Look inside our bodies and we find that everything runs on energy. To lift our left hand the brain sends an electrical energy impulse to the muscles, nerves and blood vessels involved. To read these words or to listen to them being read to us we are using energy. The unsighted could read the same words printed in braille, using the sensitivity of their fingers translated into energy sent to their brains to unscramble the message. Energy must be one of the great mysteries. The Divine Computer runs on it. It can be expressed in silence or it can manifest through the roar of a diesel engine.

We need energy to put on our clothes, wash our dishes, write our books. We then need energy to prepare our food, to eat it and digest it. Our bodies draw energy from the food. We need energy to lie in bed fighting the disharmony of disease. We need the same energy to rise up and walk, then to run. Some can climb mountains, fly aeroplanes. Others need energy to wash a child, walk a dog, go to work to earn money.

As we meditate today let us hold the mystery of energy in our minds. Make a spiritual energy pill. Take the pill. Feel your body absorbing the energy. Feel your mind absorbing it. Use this energy to combat disease. Use it to express, as well as you are able, the life force flowing through you now.

Anti-Jealousy

This meditation is to help you deal with one of the most potent and destructive forces in life – jealousy.

Go into relaxation and think for only a very brief moment of one of the major causes of jealousy in your life. If you do not ever suffer from this emotion, then firstly give thanks, and secondly put the meditation in motion on behalf of someone who does.

Once you have identified the emotion within you, take immediate action. Treat the matter as if you were dealing with a highly poisonous substance. In your mind step immediately into protective clothing. Once you are protected, proceed to isolate the substance by placing every part of it in an air-tight container. Dig, or have dug for you, a deep hole. Bury, or have buried, the poisonous substance. Cover it up completely with lovely fresh soil. Get rid of your protective clothing and concentrate on cultivating a beautifully-coloured garden over the spot. Choose all your most favourite flowers, one by one. Choose also your favourite vegetables and plant them. If you hate gardening, ask a friend to cultivate the patch for you. Trees, paths, a pond, a summer house, a section for fruit – all this and more is at your command. Stroll amongst the garden's delights, and if you so wish sit and read or meditate in your favourite seat. As you concentrate on every detail of every plant and every corner of your garden you will suddenly realize you were too busy with your positive action to think about what brought you there in the first place. Once you have overcome all those original negative thoughts, stay like that.

Ask that the theory of this meditation be built into your everyday life, now and forever

Repeat if and when necessary, choosing new and wonderful elements in your private magic garden. Enjoy it to the full.

TIME

You hear many people say, 'Time is the enemy.' In this meditation I want you to reverse that thought. Make it 'Time is valuable.' We need time to grow from the life force placed within our mother's womb to become a separate body and intelligence. We need time to grow into childhood and then adulthood. We need time to learn the great mysteries of why we are here on planet Earth and what adventures lie ahead when we are called away. We need time for now, this second, this minute, this day. Time heals. Time heals words spoken in haste. Time brings friends to visit, gives us the chance to achieve our work. Time gives us the joy of listening to music, admiring a picture, painting one.

Time is valuable, as valuable as any riches. Spend it as wisely as you can. Today as I meditate with you I am saying with you these words, 'Give me the inspiration to use time wisely. I must not waste a moment. Give me time for work well done. Time to share a moment admiring something or someone beautiful, or something beautiful in some person, or plant or animal. Give me time to meditate well, to receive and to give the best of my thought energies. I want to spend a moment in gratitude for all I have been given, all I shall be given – energy, friendship, love, Light.'

I thank you for giving time to read these words. If you are sick, use the next moment to ask for healing. If you are well, give thanks, then give time to send healing energy thoughts to your sick friends and loved ones. Spare time for the unknown to you who are also suffering. Now enjoy with me this moment of time.

Personal News Bulletins

Kill the habit of giving dreary and negative news bulletins. Sharing sorrow with a few personal friends is one thing. Going about moaning to all and sundry is another. Spread bad news and your listeners will always expect worse news. Unless it is a real emergency, disappoint them. Hand out continually negative news bulletins and you will find it is habit-forming. Your mind will be searching for new disasters to feed the demand you have created in yourself and in your audience. Stop it.

You are maybe fighting a long illness. Search about in your mind for just one positive thing – a flower smiling at you from a jam jar, a bird flying past the window, a snatch of music on the radio which pleases you, a joke that once made you smile. Put these into your news bulletins.

When I was recovering from a long and tedious illness and people asked me how I was, I said, 'Fine', and changed the subject. Sometimes I saw a glimmer of disappointment in their eyes. They wanted a gloomy news bulletin to take home and hand on. I didn't give it them. Remember, edit your own news. Stay calm. Meditate. Think UP. Take your spiritual pills. Knead your mind. Programme yourself to health.

12.
MY STORY GOES ON

IF I left the telling of my story as a healer to talk about various aspects of the work, I am now going to bring you as it were up-to-date with my story. I started this book in England, then went south to St Tropez to continue with its writing. I am now in Paris writing the final pages as I make my way back to Britain.

I have left my little wooden house on the hill at Ovingdean these last few years. The Messenger who led me there for the unfolding of my healing work then warned me in good time that changes were about to take place. Knowing the time on the hill was over, I sold the land and witnessed from afar the burning down of my house to clear the land for two new dwellings. I meanwhile was safely installed in a small brick-built bungalow nearby in Saltdean. In the distance I can glimpse the sea over the cross of my local church. I still return to Ovingdean when I can to pray in the old flint church as was my habit when in Britain. The healing work continues as ever. The hunt for a publisher for this book was long and tough. Finally, having lived through many adventures, I was speaking to my old patient and friend Pauline Lennon.

'I am celebrating my fortieth birthday and the publication of my first book on astrology,' she said cheerfully over the telephone. 'Come to the party, I'd love you to be there, and so would Socks.'

When I told Pauline about my publishing problems she generously suggested I should try her publisher. So I did, and was accepted. It seems a long time since that voice on the phone rang me seeking help for depression. Life not only handed me a wonderfully fulfilling healing experience, but also new friends who in turn handed me back a publisher all these years later. How grateful I am.

The world knows that Pauline is now called Pauline Stone, following the recent sensational book on John Lennon by Albert Goldman serialized recently in London's *Daily Mail*. I am happy to note that in her book* there is a strong accent on healing. The wheel of destiny has made another circle.

Some of us need a capital city in our lives as a place of reference and Paris is mine. I like to visit from time to time to re-equate myself with the city and also with my life. In Paris I seem to meet people and visit places which are of significance in re-aligning myself to my destiny. Perhaps the rather cynical and sometimes closed faces of the locals makes one look inside oneself for dialogue. Perhaps the inner voice is moved to speak by the poetry of the city which still presents itself in spite of the tension and the stress of modern life which spreads its parallel emotions.

Today, as on so many other days, my feet led me along the Quai Voltaire, past the Institute with its golden eighteenth century dome where generations of intellectuals have been honoured, past the Quai du Conti onto the Quai des Augustins and so on hurriedly to the wild Boulevard St Michel, here to slip through the walkabout area leading to the church of St Severin. Once inside time stands still. The beauty of the interior never ceases to move me. The tension of the city fades as I gaze once more at the rising columns holding up the gothic traceries. As I sit quietly in one of the side altars, the past and present mould into one timeless experience. I am allowed to reach deep down within myself and hold up what I find to the cleansing power of the Divine influence. I ask that the rubbish be burnt, and the essential mould be made finer. I ask to glimpse the pattern my soul is tracing, has traced and will trace on the larger canvas. In St Severin I meet myself, and have the courage so to do. My blocked ears are washed clean of trivialities, my tongue is held still, my eyes are cleared of seeing the illusion as I ask to glimpse the truth. As I touch the old stones, memories of past lives spin by, memories of the stillness I once found there. I am lost in time as I find myself.

---

*Pauline Stone, *The Astrology of Karma* The Aquarian Press, Wellingborough, 1988.

Healing Today and Tomorrow

I witnessed today a double crucifixion in a district of Paris called the Latin Quarter in a street called rue de la Harpe. A fully-loaded police wagon partly blocked the narrow street, as the peaceful crowd lined up in an orderly manner to view the proceedings. There was no rioting and no arrest . Only a few of the faces watching the spectacle showed stress, only a few muttered words of protest as Jesus, played by Willem Dafoe, was nailed mercilessly to his cross, having been beaten bloodily by the Roman soldiery. Already one cinema in Paris showing *The Last Temptation of Christ*, a film by Martin Scorcese, had been scorched by fire as protestors had demonstrated their anger at the crucifixion of the story of Christ's death and resurrection in a film which was heralded as blasphemous. In the film the healing and return to life of Lazarus took on Grand Guignol horror proportions, ever more so when he was afterwards knifed in the stomach to die again. Curiously enough I found the great story had been so deformed as to have its strength bled away as Jesus was rescued by a young girl angel to be led away into a new life on earth with wife and family. Better to have left the film to play out its own most original script in a calmer atmosphere than to have given it the huge publicity it hardly merited. Yet one can understand how some, enraged by what they considered blasphemy, were moved to crucify the film. The story of Jesus the great healer still has the power to move. But his message is rock firm, and to those who have faith, a mere film showing a trumped-up version of his temptation should in my opinion be shrugged off. After all in the Biblical story he was most sorely tempted and he resisted to fulfil his unique life. The strength of the protest demonstrates the conscience of modern man, who, in his heart, knows he has neglected to follow the great teaching. The police of the world and the soldiery are not only enforcing law and order, they are in so many disturbed areas carrying out their orders to maim and kill in the desire to enforce one religio-politico attitude on their fellow man. The essential message, love one another, is long forgotten in the quest of power, the great words are deafened by the roar of aerial bombardment and devastation.

To write about the future of healing in the terms of one healer to one or several patients might seem futile in this tumultuous setting. But write we must, and speak we must, and heal we must. If the world needs healing, so individuals must battle on to offer their individual effort. Some of us healers almost despair at times as we try to demonstrate the old message. Despair is useless, positive thought and action is useful. Healing is here to stay, and the harmony of mind, body and spirit it encourages is a huge, positive contribution to the peace of the world. If cynics and pessimists abound, healers quietly continue to radiate their calm and their hope. Healing unites, healing offers modern man's frayed nervous system respite from neurosis. Outward peace will only be established as a reflection of inner peace.

This morning, Sunday, I nearly bumped into the President of France, Monsieur Mitterand. He was striding towards me on the Quai Voltaire, deep in conversation with a companion, his long, black coat and almost round black hat accentuating the pallor of his finely-carved face, almost marble-like in its appearance. I thought of the royal heads of the country in the past, and how at one time commoners might step forward to request healing from their sovereign, a tradition which lasted until the Revolution. In England, too, the early kings were supposed by their touch to cure scrofula. Mitterand's imposing presence has at least been able up to now to cure many political diseases so that his great country, in spite of the present maddening outbreak of strikes, is taking its place in the newly-balanced Europe. As for the British royalty, they radiate an aura which manifests continuity in a changing world. Prince Charles has so often shown an interest in alternative medicine in general and spiritual healing in particular. This unofficial royal patronage has helped the case of spiritual healing enormously in Britain. More and more hospitals are giving space and time and opportunity for the patient to request and receive recognized spiritual healers as a part of their treatment. Nor are sufferers from the modern plague of AIDS denied this support, should they so desire.

If in England spiritual healing is growing up, in France it is even starting to move out of the shadows of folk-lore into the arena of media inspection. Intelligent and up-to-date books are being published about it and magazines and radio programmes give it and other alternative therapies increasing space.

In Britain for many years, officialdom in the form of the British Medical Council has issued a directive informing doctors that they cannot any longer be struck off for recommending the services of an accredited spiritual healer, provided the doctor concerned has overall control. There are also movements in Britain to have spiritual healing eventually put on the National Health Scheme. If at the time of writing this has not been achieved, a lot of discussion is going on in certain circles to this end.

Twenty years ago I do not think an article on spiritual healing written by a healer would have been a possible inclusion in a private medical journal. Last year I was invited by the National Federation of Spiritual Healers to submit such an article. I am happy to say it was accepted and printed in *Focus SE* the newsletter for the Royal College of General Practitioners, London South East Division.

As in Britain, Germany and Holland healing is looked upon with growing respect, so it is hoped by healers that this state of affairs will be accepted by the European Parliament.

Meanwhile the mysterious and wonderful power of healing flows on, oblivious of man's desire to limit, qualify, register or control. Discreetly, superbly, it goes about the work it was created to do, help man to live on planet Earth with less suffering and to move with less fear. The power of prayer knows no barrier of language, department or creed. It always has been, and always will be.

Whilst in Paris I obeyed an urge to see over those parts of the Pasteur Institute which are open to the public. This enormous institution houses laboratories actively involved in research, including, amongst many other projects, tracking down the AIDS virus, known in France as SIDA. It was the Duchess of Windsor who willed a bequest of millions of pounds from the sale of a part of her jewellery to help this particular work.

I was fascinated to visit the actual apartment lived in by Louis Pasteur and his wife, so lovingly restored to its original state by his grandson. Seeing his belongings and feeling his presence brought home to me the scholarship, dedication and humanity of the man. I was fascinated to learn as a fellow Capricorn that he was born on December 27th 1822, dying on September 28th seventy-three years later in 1895. As the piano and the pictures in his comfortable living rooms suggested, he was fond of music and paintings as well as drawing himself (mostly it seems with crayon) and he had several contemporary painters amongst his friends. Many of the *objets d'art* in his rooms were given by grateful patients. A red Gallé vase has symbols worked into the glass including some words written by another great humanist of the period, Victor Hugo.

Pasteur's private laboratory adjoining his living rooms is laid out with specimens and equipment to demonstrate his great work on defining the molecular structure as well as his work on defining and finding an antidote to the rabies vaccine, one of his great gifts to mankind and to the animal kingdom.

When Pasteur died, his wife refused to have him buried with the other French greats in the Panthéon. Instead she laid his body to rest in a beautifully-decorated chapel on the ground floor. Decorated entirely with shining mosaic, its Italianate form features beautiful illustrations representing all the facets of his work. On the ceiling over his tomb are the words taken from his address on being received into the Academy. They speak for the man.

> Blessed is the man who lives and works
> For a God, for an ideal of beauty,
> The ideal of Art, the ideal of Science,
> The ideal of home and country,
> The ideal of the virtues of the gospel.

I came away from my visit with the feeling that I had paid homage to a man whose spirit continues to research in the next world and whose vitality continues to inspire scientists, doctors and all those working for the healing cause on more than one time level. I for one, am grateful.

Back in Saltdean I took the almost complete manuscript of this book out of my travelling case and dropped it onto my writing table.

Tackling my mail, I read the calls of distress, the good news of the healed and happy mixed with the cries for help. I met the grandmother of little Mark, aged five. Three years ago this anxious grandmother told me of his chronic enteritis causing malabsorption of food and the consequent slow development of his physique. It was a pale boy I saw then on his photo from

Australia. Now, hurrah, he has responded to the powers of absent healing, and his photo shows a sturdy boy eating a hamburger and chips. Mark is out of trouble and Gran gives me a kiss.

Although I often take communion at midnight at the great ecumenical Mass at nearby Worth Abbey, this year I celebrated the birth of that special child at Ovingdean's St Wulfren's, where I have worshipped for many years. I thought of little Mark all those miles away in Melbourne, Australia, and gave thanks.

Amongst the stream of Christmas cards I received two invitations which I chose to follow up. The first brought me to visit Michael Endacott who, as deputy head of the Institute of Contemporary Medicine, wanted to show me over their splendid Adam's building nearly opposite the BBC in London's Portland Place. Later Michael was to ask for my opinion after a lecture by intermediary negotiators to government, on standardizing codes of behaviour in readiness for continuing talks with European governments. I absorbed the significance of analysing skills, techniques and codes of conduct concerning many recognized alternative therapies. The talks and negotiations go on. Meanwhile in Britain lists of accredited healing sources are now on display in the waiting rooms of co-operating doctors.

The other invitation was to meet and experience the mediumship of a man called Leslie Flint. For over fifty years, Leslie has demonstrated his remarkable direct-voice mediumship under private or public conditions. Locked and gagged into glass cabinets, photographed by infra-red cameras, filmed, recorded, examined, tested by the experts – the voices speaking loud and clear from a site just above and to one side of his head still come. As Leslie has now retired from his great life's work it was a privilege to be invited to sit in on one of his increasingly rare private séances, something I had for years wanted to attend.

As we sat in the darkened room and waited for the communicative voices to start speaking from another time level, past the barrier we refer to as death, I marvelled when I first heard the voice of Mickey, his guide, almost shouting his contact from the other side. I have since attended more than one séance of Leslie's but nothing is more remarkable than one's first hearing the voices. It did not surprise me to hear a French communicator telling me about my healing confederates who are helping my healing work from the other side. A group of 'dead' scientists and doctors have, I am told, interested themselves in my work here. Surprised? No. Grateful? Yes.

Never did I dream that a few months later Leslie himself should contact me for healing. I had meanwhile read his book *Voices in the Dark* published by Psychic Press, (originally by Macmillan), to learn about his remarkable career, linked with Rudolph Valentino and with Mae West, whose presence at the Savoy Hotel those years ago demonstrated her interest in matters spiritual and psychic, and who had often invited Leslie out to Hollywood to work for her. Since her death, Leslie has continued to stay in LA for several months each year. This year was nearly the exception, owing to bad health. Thus I was contacted.

As I greeted Leslie in my healing sanctuary I could sense what he told me, that he was in great pain, not only in the neck and chest but also in his shoulder area, pain which made him feel ill. He felt in no state to travel and was about to consider cancelling his trip to LA. The next day, after one treatment, he felt better. With all the pain gone he flew off shortly afterwards for his yearly visit to Hollywood.

As a result of the questioning of his friends in Hollywood as to how he was well enough to travel and enjoy his holiday, I have had an invitation which I have happily accepted. So as a direct consequence of my healing hands I am flying off to Hollywood to stay within a short distance of Paramount Studios, so near to where both Valentino and Mae West lived and worked.

Once more I am grateful I had the courage those years ago to accept my healing powers, and to obey the voice telling me to write this book. And what better way to end it, than to say with joy and wonder, 'I'm off for a visit to Hollywood! Los Angeles, here I come.'

INDEX

Alleyne, John, 47
Armfield, Stuart, 50
Ashton, Sir Frederick, 64

Bacon, Charlotte, 28, 48
   Gwen, 38–9, 158
   Lewis, 31–6, 39
   Mai, 23
   Patsy, 21, 26, 37
   Patrick, 38
   Sir Roger Sewell, 21, 32, 42, 61–2
   Sewell, 27
   Sydney, 27
Baddeley, Hermione, 97–9
Bardot, Brigitte, 164–5
Bassey, Shirley, 183
Bath, Daphne, 50
Brave Spirit, 82, 103–5
Bray, George, 50
Brooke, Clive, 22
   Faith, 22

Cade, Maxwell, (Report by), 125
Chardin, Teilhard de, 128
Chevalier, Maurice, 140
Chulah, Prince of Siam, 50
Clements, Sir John, 62
Colette, 100, 142
Coward, Sir Noël, 58, 140
Cry for the Moon, 52

Dain, Yvonne Le, 33

Dean, Sir Basil, 28
Dietrich, Marlene, 116–18
Dolly Sisters, The, 25
Dresdel, Sonia, 41
Dukes, Ashley, 41
Duncan, Raymond, 58

Edinburgh, His Royal Highness, Duke of, 27
Ellis, Mary, 52
Elizabeth, Her Majesty the Queen Mother, 27
Endacott, Michael, 195

'Fairways', 90–7
Festival of Mind and Body, Olympia, 124
Fielding, Harold, 56
   Ian, 50
Flint, Leslie, 24, 195–6

Garland, Judy, 139–41
Gibbons, Carol, 19
Glastonbury Abbey, 47
Granger, Stewart, 39
Grappelli, Stephane, 99
Greene, Nigel, 79–81

Hall, Sir Harry, 23
   Lady Marie, 23–6
Hammond, Kay, 63
Hill, Clive, 106
Holistic Healing, Conference, 114

Jesus, 128–9, 191
Jung, C. G., 126
Juvenal, Colette de, 100

Kaye, Danny, 51
Kennedy family, 20
Kent, Jean, 56
Kilner, Dr, 121
Kirlian, Semyon, 121–2
   Valentina, 122
Knight, Peter, 56

Leigh, Vivien, 62–6
Leighton, Marguerite, 51
Lennon, Pauline, 111–13, 190
London University, 19

Mackenzie, Nan, 40–1
Maugham, Robin, Lord, 57, 101–2
Minelli, Liza, 141
Mitterand, President, 192
Mountbatten, Lady, 33

National Federation of Spiritual Healers, 109, 114
Novello, Ivor, 39, 52

Oberon, Merle, Lady Korda, 22
Odell, Anni and John, 167

Paris, 58–9, 192
Pasteur Institute, 193–4
Pasteur, Louis, 193–4
Piaf, Edith, 59
Point of View, 62
Portman, Eric, 50
Psychic News, 40, 111–12

Queen Elizabeth Hospital, Birmingham, 19

Quinlivan, Jack, 86
   Nellie, 86–9

Rampling, Charlotte, 154–6
Rattigan, Terence, 51
Robson, Dame Flora, 58
Rugby School, 19–20

Saint Tropez, 61–2, 142
Sand, George, 58
Savoy Hotel, London, 19–20, 23–4
Scantlebury, Tony, 109–11
Selfridge, Gordon, 24
She Smiled at Me, 55, 61
Sinden, Donald, 52
Snellgrove, Brian, 123
Sommerville, J. Baxter, 55
Southcombe, Brian, 154–6
Strachey, Jack, 57
Suvretta House, St Moritz, 20
Syms, Joanna, 15–17

Toms, Mrs Hilda, 44, 46, 47
Tripp, Jack, 61

Vernon, Anne, 154
Volkova, Vera, 38

Walton, Sir William and Lady, 57
West, Mae, 23–4
Weymouth, Viscount Alexander, 50
Wilde, Marty, 61
Wilkinson, Sir George and Lady, 27
Woman's Own, 113

Young, Dr (lung specialist), 32, 43, 48